AN INDEX
ENGLISH COUNTRY
HOUSES

compiled by

Cliff Webb

Published by the Society of Genealogists
1999

Published by
Society of Genealogists
14 Charterhouse Buildings
Goswell Road
London EC1M 7BA
Registered Charity No. 233701

ISBN 1 85951 702 1

Introduction

This is an index of 5,719 English country houses which were in existence in the 1920s and 1930s. The index includes Monmouthshire and the Channel Islands. It does not include the main part of Wales, Scotland or Ireland.

It gives the name of the house, and the place and county (abbreviated using the 'Chapman County Codes') in which it is or was situated. The list is almost entirely compiled from Kelly's County Directories which gave a 'List of the Principal Seats in ...'. For the area of the old London County Council, where Kelly's Directories do not list substantial houses in the same way, recourse has been made to Pevsner's Buildings of England series; such houses have been allocated to their pre-1800 parish, and pre-1889 county. London is therefore represented here on a different basis from the rest of the country.

It can be a most difficult tasks to identify the location of a country house, where only the name is known. Postcards of such houses, for example, are frequently identified merely with the name of the house, without parish or county. Family historians, having such material addressed from or to an ancestor will be able to locate the house concerned. They will also be able to look up places of interest and find the owners of them in the early twentieth century. Again, it can be very difficult to trace the movements of servants in these houses, who might be moved to other properties of their employer. By looking up the original directory the family who owned the house at the time may be identified, which is a good starting point for further research.

The list is strictly alphabetical, except that 'The' has been placed in brackets after the main components of the name of the house, and the counties are those given in the list rather than those which later reorganisation may have placed a house in. The following list of counties shows the code, and also the Kelly's Directory edition which was used in each case.

Bdf = Bedfordshire 1940
Brk = Berkshire 1939
Bkm = Buckinghamshire 1935
Cam = Cambridgeshire 1925
Channel Islands = 1931
Chs = Cheshire 1928
Con = Cornwall 1939
Cul = Cumberland 1929
Dby = Derbyshire 1932
Dev = Devon 1939
Dor = Dorset 1931
Dur = Durham 1938
Ess = Essex 1937
Gls = Gloucestershire 1927
Ham = Hampshire 1931
Hef = Herefordshire 1941
Hrt = Hertfordshire 1937
Hun = Huntingdonshire 1936
Ken = Kent 1934
Lan = Lancashire 1924
Lei = Leicestershire 1932
Lin = Lincolnshire 1937

Mdx = Middlesex 1937
Mon = Monmouthshire 1937
Nfk = Norfolk 1925
Nth = Northamptonshire 1936
Nbl = Northumberland 1938
Ntt = Nottinghamshire 1932
Oxf = Oxfordshire 1928
Rut = Rutland 1932
Sal = Shropshire 1941
Som = Somerset 1931
Sts = Staffordshire 1940
Sfk = Suffolk 1925
Sry = Surrey 1938
Ssx = Sussex 1934
War = Warwickshire 1932
Wes = Westmorland 1929
Wil = Wiltshire 1931
Wor = Worcestershire 1932
Ery = Yorkshire, East Riding 1937
Nry = Yorkshire, North Riding 1937
Wry = Yorkshire, West Riding 1936

Cliff Webb January 1999

INDEX OF ENGLISH COUNTRY HOUSES

Abberley Hall, Abberley, Wor
Abberton Hall, Abberton, Wor
Abberton Manor, Abberton, Ess
Abbey Manor, Evesham, Wor
Abbey (The), Aston Abbots, Bkm
Abbey (The), Much Wenlock, Sal
Abbey (The), Storrington, Ssx
Abbeystead, Over Wyresdale, Lan
Abbot's Hall, Shalford, Ess
Abbot's Hall, Stowmarket, Sfk
Abbot's Wood, Barrow in Furness, Lan
Abbots Langley Manor House, Abbots Langley, Hrt
Abbots Moss, Marton, Chs
Abbots Ripton Hall, Abbots Ripton, Hun
Abbotsbury Castle, Abbotsbury, Dor
Abbotsfield, Wiveliscombe, Som
Abbotsham Court, Abbotsham, Dev
Abbotsleigh, Wivelsfield, Ssx
Abbotswood, Lower Swell, Gls
Abbotts Barton, Winchester, Ham
Abinger Hall, Abinger, Sry
Abington Hall, Abington, Cam
Abnalls, Burntwood, Sts
Ackworth Grange, Ackworth, Yks
Ackworth House, East Bergholt, Sfk
Ackworth Park, Ackworth, Yks
Acomb House, St John Lee, Nbl
Acryse Place, Acrise, Ken
Acton Burnell Park, Acton Burnell, Sal
Acton House, Felton, Nbl
Acton Place, Acton, Sfk
Acton Scott Hall, Acton Scott, Sal
Adbury Park, Burghclere, Ham
Adderbury House, Adderbury, Oxf
Adderley Hall, Adderley, Sal
Adderstone Hall, Adderstone, Nbl
Addington House, Addington, Bkm
Addington Manor, Addington, Bkm
Addington Manor, Great Addington, Nth
Adhurst St Mary, Sheet, Ham
Adlestrop House, Adlestrop, Gls
Adlington Hall, Adlington, Chs
Admington Hall, Quinton, Gls
Admiral's House, Hampstead, Mdx
Adsdean, Westbourne, Ssx
Adstock Manor, Adstock, Bkm
Adwell House, Adwell, Oxf
Afton Manor, Freshwater, Ham
Aiskew House, Bedale, Yks
Aisthorpe House, Aisthorpe, Lin
Albrighton Hall, Shrewsbury, Sal
Albury Hall, Albury, Hrt
Albury Park, Albury, Sry
Albyns, Stapleford Abbots, Ess
Alconbury House, Alconbury, Hun
Aldborough Hall, Aldborough, Nfk
Aldborough Hall, Aldborough, Yks
Aldborough Manor, Aldborough, Yks
Aldburgh Hall, Masham, Yks
Aldby Park, Bossall, Yks

Aldcliffe Hall, Aldcliffe, Lan
Aldenham Park, Morville, Sal
Alderbrook Park, Cranleigh, Sry
Alderbury House, Alderbury, Wil
Aldercar Hall, Codnor Park, Dby
Alderholt Park, Alderholt, Dor
Alderley Park, Alderley, Chs
Aldermaston Court, Aldermaston, Brk
Aldershaw, Wall, Sts
Alderwasley Hall, Alderwasley, Dby
Aldingham Hall, Aldingham, Lan
Aldington Court, Thurnham, Ken
Aldon, Yeovil, Som
Aldridge Court, Aldridge, Sts
Aldringham House, Aldringham, Sfk
Aldwark Manor, Alne, Yks
Aldwick Court, Blagdon, Som
Aldwick Place, Aldwick, Ssx
Aldworth House, Lurgashall, Ssx
Alford House, Alford, Som
Alfoxton House, Holford, Som
Alfreton Park, Alfreton, Dby
Algars Manor, Iron Acton, Gls
Alkrington Hall, Middleton, Lan
Allanbay, Binfield, Brk
Allenheads Hall, Allenheads, Nbl
Allensmore Court, Allensmore, Hef
Alleron, Loddiswell, Dev
Allerthorpe Hall, Allerthorpe, Yks
Allerton Manor, Allerton Mauleverer, Yks
Allesley Hall, Allesley, War
Allexton Hall, Allexton, Lei
Allington Castle, Allington, Ken
Allington Hall, Allington, Lin
Alne Hall, Alne, Yks
Alnwick Castle, Alnwick, Nbl
Alresford Hall, Alresford, Ess
Alscot Park House, Preston on Stour, War
Alscot Park, Preston on Stour, Gls
Alsprings, Great Harwood, Lan
Althorp, Althorp, Nth
Alton Manor, Idridgehay, Dby
Alton Pancras Manor House, Alton Pancras, Dor
Alwalton Hall, Alwalton, Hun
Amberley Court, Amberley, Gls
Amesbury Abbey, Amesbury, Wil
Amington Hall, Amington, War
Ammerdown Park, Kilmersdon, Som
Ampfield House, Ampfield, Ham
Ampney Park, Ampney Crucis, Gls
Amport House, Amport, Ham
Ampthill House, Ampthill, Bdf
Ampthill Park, Ampthill, Bdf
Ampton Hall, Ampton, Sfk
Anderson Manor, Anderson, Dor
Angerton Hall, Hartburn, Nbl
Anglesey Abbey, Lode, Cam
Anmer Hall, Anmer, Nfk
Annan, East Hoathly, Ssx
Annery House, Monkleigh, Dev

1

INDEX OF ENGLISH COUNTRY HOUSES

Annesley Park, Annesley, Ntt
Anningsley Park, Chertsey, Sry
Anstey Manor, Alton, Ham
Anstie Grange, Dorking, Sry
Antony House, Antony, Con
Apethorpe Hall, Apethorpe, Nth
Apley Castle, Wellington, Sal
Apley Park, Stockton, Sal
Apperley Court, Deerhurst, Gls
Apple Tree Court, Lyndhurst, Ham
Appleby Castle, Appleby, Wes
Appleton Hall, Appleton, Chs
Appleton Hall, Appleton le Moors, Yks
Appleton House, Appleton, Nfk
Apsley House, Westminster, Mdx
Apton Hall, Canewdon, Ess
Aqualate Hall, Forton, Sts
ArborfieldHall, Arborfield, Brk
Arbury Hall, Nuneaton, War
Arclid Hall, Arclid, Chs
Arcot Hall, Cramlington, Nbl
Ardeley Bury, Ardeley, Hrt
Arden Hall, Hawnby, Yks
Arderne Hall, Eaton, Chs
Areley Hall, Areley Kings, Wor
Argoed (The), Penallt, Mon
Arkendale Hall, Arkendale, Yks
Arle Bury, New Alresford, Ham
Arley Hall, Aston by Budworth, Chs
Arlington Court, Arlington, Dev
Arlington Manor, Chieveley, Brk
Armathwaite Castle, Armathwaite, Cul
Armathwaite Hall, Bassenthwaite, Cul
Armsworth House, Alresford, Ham
Arncliffe Hall, Ingleby Arncliffe, Yks
Arthington Hall, Arthington, Yks
Arthingworth Manor, Arthingworth, Nth
Arthur's Seat, Caterham, Sry
Arundel Castle, Arundel, Ssx
Ascot Place, Winkfield, Brk
Ascott, Ascott, Bkm
Ash, Iddesleigh, Dev
Ash Mount, Haworth, Yks
Ashborne Hill House, Newbold Pacey, War
Ashbrook Towers, Church Minshull, Chs
Ashburnham Place, Ashburnham, Ssx
Ashby Hall, Ashby de la Launde, Lin
Ashby Hall, Ashby St Mary, Nfk
Ashby St Ledgers Manor House, Ashby St Ledgers, Nth
Ashchurch House, Ashchurch, Gls
Ashcombe Park, Cheddleton, Sts
Ashdown Park, Ashbury, Brk
Ashe High House, Campsea Ashe, Sfk
Ashe Park, Ashe, Ham
Ashe Warren House, Ashe, Ham
Ashendene, Bayford, Hrt
Ashenhurst Hall, Onecote, Sts
Asherne, Morchard Bishop, Dev
Ashfield House, Otley, Yks

Ashfield Lodge, Great Ashfield, Sfk
Ashfold, Slaugham, Ssx
Ashford Carbonell Manor House, Ashford Carbonell, Sal
Ashford Court, Ashford Carbonell, Sal
Ashford Hall, Ashford Bowdler, Sal
Ashford Hall, Ashford, Dby
Ashgate Lodge, Brampton, Dby
Ashlands (The), Ilston on the Hill, Lei
Ashley Bank, Newbiggin on Lune, Wes
Ashley Combe, Porlock, Som
Ashley Green, Rydal and Loughrigg, Wes
Ashley Manor, Charlton Kings, Gls
Ashlyns Hall, Great Berkhamsted, Hrt
Ashmans Hall, Barsham, Sfk
Ashton, Chaffcombe, Som
Ashton Court, Long Ashton, Som
Ashton Hall, Ashton with Stodday, Lan
Ashton Hayes, Ashton Hayes, Chs
Ashton House, Ashton Keynes, Wil
Ashton Park, Ashton, Lan
Ashton Wold, Oundle, Nth
Ashurst Park, Ashurst, Ken
Ashwell Hall, Ashwell, Rut
Ashwellthorpe Hall, Ashwellthorpe, Nfk
Ashwick Grove, Ashwick, Som
Ashwicke Hall, Marshfield, Gls
Ashwicken Hall, Ashwicken, Nfk
Aske, Easby, Yks
Askerton Castle, Askerton, Cul
Askham Grange, Askham Richard, Yks
Aspenden Hall, Aspenden, Hrt
Aspley Hall, New Radford, Ntt
Aspley House, Aspley Guise, Bdf
Assington Hall, Assington, Sfk
Astbury Hall, Chelmarsh, Sal
Asthall Manor House, Asthall, Oxf
Astle Hall, Chelford, Chs
Astley Abbotts, Astley Abbotts, Sal
Astley Castle, Astley, War
Astley Hall, Astley, Wor
Astley Hall, Chorley, Lan
Aston Bury, Aston, Hrt
Aston Hall, Aston, Yks
Aston Hall, Church Aston, Sal
Aston Hall, Oswestry, Sal
Aston Hall, Shifnal, Sal
Aston House, Aston, Hrt
Aston House, Aston Rowant, Oxf
Aston Lodge, Aston by Sutton, Chs
Astrop House, King's Sutton, Nth
Aswarby Park, Aswarby, Lin
Aswardby Hall, Aswardby, Lin
Atcombe Court, Woodchester, Gls
Athelhampton Hall, Athelhampton, Dor
Atherstone Hall, Atherstone, War
Attingham Park, Atcham, Sal
Attleborough Lodge, Attleborough, Nfk
Auberies, Bulmer, Ess
Auckland Castle, Bishop Auckland, Dur

INDEX OF ENGLISH COUNTRY HOUSES

Audley End, Saffron Walden, Ess
Audleys Wood, Cliddesden, Ham
Augill Castle, Stainmore, Wes
Austin Canons, Kempston, Bdf
Austwick Hall, Austwick, Yks
Avening Court, Avening, Gls
Avington House, Avington, Ham
Avishays House, Chaffcombe, Som
Avon Carrow, Avon Dassett, War
Avon Castle, Ringwood, Ham
Avonbank, Wick, Wor
Avranche, St Lawrence, Jersey
Awbridge Danes, Awbridge, Ham
Aynho Park, Aynho, Nth
Ayot Bury, Ayot St Peter, Hrt
Ayot Place, Ayot St Peter, Hrt
Ayot St Lawrence House, Ayot St Lawrence, Hrt
Ayston Hall, Ayston, Rut
Ayton Firs, Ayton, Yks
Azerley Chase, Azerley, Yks

Babergh Hall, Great Waldingfield, Sfk
Babington House, Babington, Som
Babraham Hall, Babraham, Cam
Babworth Hall, Babworth, Ntt
Backford Hall, Backford, Chs
Backwell Hill House, Backwell, Som
Bacres, Hambleden, Bkm
Bacton Grange, Bacton, Hef
Badby House, Badby, Nth
Baddesley Clinton Hall, Baddesley Clinton, War
Badger Hall, Badger, Sal
Badgeworth Court, Badgeworth, Gls
Badgworth Court, Weare, Som
Badminton House, Badminton, Gls
Badmondisfield Hall, Wickhambrook, Sfk
Badsworth Hall, Badsworth, Yks
Badwell Ash Hall, Badwell Ash, Sfk
Bagborough House, West Bagborough, Som
Bagden Hall, Scissett, Yks
Bagendon House, Bagendon, Gls
Baggrave Hall, Baggrave, Lei
Bagshot Park, Windlesham, Sry
Bagthorpe Hall, Bagthorpe, Nfk
Bailiffscourt, Climping, Ssx
Bainton House, Bainton, Nth
Balcombe Place, Balcombe, Ssx
Balderstone Grange, Balderstone, Lan
Baldon House, Baldon Marsh, Oxf
Baldslow Place, Westfield, Ssx
Balls Park, Hertford, Hrt
Bamburgh Castle, Bamburgh, Nbl
Bangors Park, Iver, Bkm
Bank Hall, Bretherton, Lan
Bank Hall, Chapel en le Frith, Dby
Bank House, Acklington, Nbl
Banks Fee, Longborough, Gls
Banwell Abbey, Banwell, Som
Banwell Castle, Banwell, Som
Barbon Manor, Barbon, Wes

Barcote Manor, Buckland, Brk
Bardon Hall, Bardon, Lei
Bardsea Hall, Bardsea, Lan
Bardwell Manor, Bardwell, Sfk
Barford Hill, Barford, War
Barham Court, Teston, Ken
Barham House, East Hoathly, Ssx
Barkby Hall, Barkby, Lei
Barkfold House, Kirdford, Ssx
Barking Hall, Barking, Sfk
Barkston Towers, Sherburn in Elmet, Yks
Barlborough Hall, Barlborough, Dby
Barlborough House, Barlborough, Dby
Barley Wood, Wrington, Som
Barleythorpe Hall, Barleythorpe, Rut
Barmer Hall, Barmer, Nfk
Barmoor Castle, Lowick, Nbl
Barnacre Lodge, Barnacre, Lan
Barnardiston Hall, Barnardiston, Sfk
Barnborough Hall, Barnborough, Yks
Barnby Manor, Barnby in the Willows, Ntt
Barnett Hill, Wonersh, Sry
Barningham Hall, Barningham Winter, Nfk
Barningham Park, Barningham, Yks
Barnjet, West Barming, Ken
Barns (The), Fenlake, Bdf
Barnsley Park, Barnsley, Gls
Barnwell Castle, Barnwell, Nth
Baron's Down, Brompton Regis, Som
Barrells Park, Ullenhall, War
Barrington Court, Barrington, Som
Barrington Hall, Barrington, Cam
Barrington Hall, Hatfield, Ess
Barrington Park House, Great Barrington, Gls
Barrock Park, Petteril Crooks, Cul
Barrow Court, Barrow Gurney, Som
Barrow Green Court, Oxted, Sry
Barrow Hall, Barrow on Humber, Lin
Barrow Hall, Barrow on Trent, Dby
Barrow Hill, Rocester, Sts
Bartle Hall, Woodplumpton, Lan
Bartlow House, Bartlow, Cam
Barton Abbey, Steeple Barton, Oxf
Barton Bendish Hall, Barton Bendish, Nfk
Barton Court, Colwall, Hef
Barton Court, Kintbury, Brk
Barton Grange, Pitminster, Som
Barton Hall, Barton Blount, Dby
Barton Hartshorn Manor, Barton Hartshorn, Bkm
Barton House, Barton on the Heath, War
Barton House, Morchard Bishop, Dev
Barton Mere, Pakenham, Sfk
Barwell Court, Kingston, Sry
Barwick House, Barwick, Nfk
Barwick House, Barwick, Som
Barwythe, Studham, Bdf
Basford Hall, Cheddleton, Sts
Basildon Park, Basildon, Brk
Basing Park, Froxfield, Ham
Basset Down House, Lydiard Tregoze, Wil

Bassett Wood, Southampton, Ham
Batchelors, Shipley, Ssx
Bathford Manor House, Bathford, Som
Batsford Park, Batsford, Gls
Battlefields (The), Cold Ashton, Gls
Bawdeswell Hall, Bawdeswell, Nfk
Bawdsey Manor, Bawdsey, Sfk
Bawtry Hall, Bawtry, Yks
Baxenden House, Baxenden, Lan
Bay House, Gosport, Ham
Baydon Manor, Ramsbury, Wil
Bayfield Hall, Bayfield, Nfk
Bayford Lodge, Stoke Trister, Som
Bayfordbury, Bayford, Hrt
Bayham Abbey, Lamberhurst, Ken
Baynards Park, Cranleigh, Sry
Baynton House, East Coulston, Wil
Bayons Manor, Tealby, Lin
Baythorne Park, Birdbrook, Ess
Beacon Banks, Husthwaite, Yks
Beacon Hall, Staplefield, Ssx
Beacon Hill, Martlesham, Sfk
Beamhurst Hall, Checkley, Sts
Beaminster Manor House, Beaminster, Dor
Beamish Park, Tanfield, Dur
Beanlands Park, Irthington, Cul
Beara Court, Black Torrington, Dev
Beauchief Hall, Beauchief, Dby
Beaufront Castle, St John Lee, Nbl
Beaumanor Park, Beaumanor, Lei
Beaumont Manor, Cheshunt, Hrt
Beauport, Hollington, Ssx
Beaurepaire Park, Sherborne St John, Ham
Beauvale House, Moorgreen, Ntt
Becca Hall, Aberford, Yks
Beck Foot, Winton, Wes
Beckbury Hall, Beckbury, Sal
Beckenham Place, Lewisham, Ken
Beckfoot, Bampton, Wes
Beckford Hall, Beckford, Gls
Beckington Castle, Beckington, Som
Bedale Hall, Bedale, Yks
Bedstone Court, Bedstone, Sal
Bedwell Park, Essendon, Hrt
Beech Hill House, Beech Hill, Brk
Beech Hill, Morchard Bishop, Dev
Beech Hill Park, Waltham Abbey, Ess
Beeches (The), Moore, Chs
Beechfield, Corsham, Wil
Beechland, Newick, Ssx
Beechwood House, Copythorne, Ham
Beechwood, Marlow, Bkm
Beechwood Park, Flamstead, Hrt
Beechwood, Sparkwell, Dev
Beedingwood, Lower Beeding, Ssx
Beenham Court, Woodlands, Ham
Beenham House, Beenham, Brk
Beesthorpe Hall, Beesthorpe, Ntt
Beeston Hall, Beeston St Andrew, Nfk
Beeston Hall, Beeston St Lawrence, Nfk

Beeston Regis Hall, Beeston Regis, Nfk
Belair, Dulwich, Sry
Belfield House, Fulham, Mdx
Belford Hall, Belford, Nbl
Belhus, Aveley, Ess
Bell Hall, Belbroughton, Wor
Bell Hall, Naburn, Yks
Bellister Castle, Haltwhistle, Nbl
Bellshill, Lucker, Nbl
Belmont, Christchurch, Mon
Belmont Hall, Great Budworth, Chs
Belmont Hall, Ipstones, Sts
Belmont, Throwley, Ken
Belmore House, Upham, Ham
Belringham, Sutton Valence, Ken
Belsay Castle, Bolam, Nbl
Belswardyne Hall, Cressage, Sal
Belton House, Belton and Manthorpe, Lin
Belvoir Castle, Belvoir, Lei
Benacre Hall, Benacre, Sfk
Benchams, Harpford, Dev
Benhall Lodge, Benhall, Sfk
Benham Park, Stockcross, Brk
Beningbrough Hall, Newton upon Ouse, Yks
Benington Park, Benington, Hrt
Benthall Hall, Benthall, Sal
Bentley Manor, Bentley Pauncefoot, Wor
Bentworth Hall, Bentworth, Ham
Benwell Tower, Newcastle, Nbl
Beoley Hall, Beoley, Wor
Berden Hall, Berden, Ess
Bere Court, Pangbourne, Brk
Bere Hill, Whitchurch, Ham
Berechurch Hall, Colchester, Ess
Bereleigh House, East Meon, Ham
Bergh Apton Cottage, Bergh Apton, Nfk
Bergh Apton Manor House, Bergh Apton, Nfk
Berkeley Castle, Berkeley, Gls
Berkeley, Dunkirk, Ken
Berkhamsted Place, Great Berkhamsted, Hrt
Berkley House, Berkley, Som
Berkswell Hall, Berkswell, War
Bernithan Court, Llangarron, Hef
Berrington Hall, Eye, Hef
Berry Hall, Solihull, War
Berrydown Court, Overton, Ham
Berwick House, Berwick, Sal
Beryl, Wells, Som
Besselsleigh Manor, Besselsleigh, Brk
Bessingham Manor House, Bessingham, Nfk
Besthorpe Hall, Besthorpe, Nfk
Bestwood Lodge, Bestwood Park, Ntt
Betchworth House, Betchworth, Sry
Betley Court, Betley, Sts
Bevere House, North Claines, Wor
Bickham House, Kenn, Dev
Bickleigh Castle, Bickleigh, Dev
Bicton House, Bicton, Dev
Bidborough Court, Bidborough, Ken
Biddesden House, Ludgershall, Wil

Biddick Hall, Burnmoor, Dur
Biddlesden Park, Biddlesden, Bkm
Biddlestone Hall, Alwinton, Nbl
Bifrons, Patrixbourne, Ken
Bigadon, Buckfastleigh, Dev
Biggin Hall, Lower Benefield, Nth
Biggins (The), Kirkby Lonsdale, Wes
Bighton Wood, Bighton, Ham
Bigland Hall, Haverthwaite, Lan
Bignell House, Bicester, Oxf
Bignor Park, Bignor, Ssx
Bilbrough Manor, Bilbrough, Yks
Bill Hill, Hurst, Brk
Billesley Manor, Billesley, War
Billing Hall, Great Billing, Nth
Billington Manor, Billington, Bdf
Bilsborough, Henfield, Ssx
Bilsby House, Bilsby, Lin
Bilton Hall, Bilton, Yks
Bindon, Langford Budville, Som
Bineham, Chailey, Ssx
Binfield Court, Binfield, Brk
Binfield Lodge, Binfield, Brk
Binfield Manor, Binfield, Brk
Binfield Park, Binfield, Brk
Bingham's Melcombe, Bingham, Dor
Binnegar Hall, East Stoke, Dor
Binsted-Wyck, Binsted, Ham
Birch Hall, Birch, Ess
Birch House, Much Birch, Hef
Birchamp House, Newland, Gls
Birdingbury Hall, Birdingbury, War
Birdsall House, Birdsall, Yks
Birkin House, Stinsford, Dor
Birklands, Kendal, Wes
Birthwaite Hall, Darton, Yks
Birtles Hall, Birtles, Chs
Birtles Old Hall, Birtles, Chs
Biscathorpe House, Gayton le Wold, Lin
Bisham Abbey, Bisham, Brk
Bishop Oak, Wolsingham, Dur
Bishop's Court, Sowton, Dev
Bishop's Hall, Lambourne, Ess
Bishop's Manor, Southwell, Ntt
Bishopstrow House, Bishopstrow, Wil
Bishopswood, Bishopswood, Hef
Bishopthorpe Palace, Bishopthorpe, Yks
Bishton Hall, Colwich, Sts
Bisterne, Bisterne, Ham
Bitterley Court, Bitterley, Sal
Bittiscombe Manor, Upton, Som
Blachford, Cornwood, Dev
Black Hall, Avonwick, Dev
Blackbrooke, Skenfrith, Mon
Blackdown House, Lodsworth, Ssx
Blackheath, Friston, Sfk
Blackland House, Calne, Wil
Blacklands Hall, Cavendish, Sfk
Blacklands, Sparkwell, Dev
Blackmoor, Blackmoor, Ham

Blackwater, Minstead, Ham
Blackwell Grange, Darlington, Dur
Blagdon Hall, Stannington, Nbl
Blaisdon Hall, Blaisdon, Gls
Blake Hall, Bobbingworth, Ess
Blakeshall Hall, Wolverley, Wor
Blakesley Hall, Blakesley, Nth
Blakesware, Wareside, Hrt
Blankney Hall, Blankney, Lin
Blatherwycke Park, Blatherwycke, Nth
Blenheim Palace, Blenheim, Oxf
Blenkinsopp Castle, Greenhead, Nbl
Blenkinsopp Hall, Haltwhistle, Nbl
Bletchington Park, Bletchington, Oxf
Bletchley Park, Bletchley, Bkm
Blickling Hall, Blickling, Nfk
Blidworth Dale, Blidworth, Ntt
Blindburn, Birtley, Nbl
Blithfield Hall, Blithfield, Sts
Blofield Hall, Blofield, Nfk
Blofield House, Blofield, Nfk
Blounts Court, Potterne, Wil
Bloxholm Hall, Bloxholm, Lin
Bloxworth House, Bloxworth, Dor
Bluegates, Wherstead, Sfk
Blunham House, Blunham, Bdf
Blyborough Hall, Blyborough, Lin
Blyth Hall, Blyth, Ntt
Blyth Hall, Shustoke, War
Blythe Hall, Lathom, Lan
Boarzell, Flimwell, Ssx
Bockelton Court, Bockelton, Wor
Boconnoc, Boconnoc, Con
Boddington Manor, Boddington, Gls
Bodicote Grange, Bodicote, Oxf
Bodicote House, Bodicote, Oxf
Bolam Hall, Bolam, Nbl
Boldre Grange, Boldre, Ham
Bolebroke, Hartfield, Ssx
Bolesworth Castle, Broxton, Chs
Bolnore, Cuckfield, Ssx
Bolsover Castle, Bolsover, Dby
Bolton Abbey, Bolton Abbey, Yks
Bolton Hall, Bolton by Bowland, Yks
Bolton Hall, Edlingham, Nbl
Bolton Hall, Wensley, Yks
Bolton House, Hampstead, Mdx
Bolwick Hall, Marsham, Nfk
Bonningtons, Stanstead Abbotts, Hrt
Boothby Hall, Boothby Graffoe, Lin
Boothby Hall, Boothby Pagnell, Lin
Borde Hill, Cuckfield, Ssx
Borden Wood, Chithurst, Ssx
Bordesley Hall, Alvechurch, Wor
Boreatton Hall, Baschurch, Sal
Borrenthwaite, Stainmore, Wes
Borwick Hall, Warton, Lan
Bosahan, St Anthony in Meneage, Con
Bosbury House, Bosbury, Hef
Boskenna, St Buryan, Con

Bosmere Hall, Creeting St Mary, Sfk
Bossall Hall, Bossall, Yks
Bossington House, Bossington, Ham
Bostock Hall, Bostock, Chs
Boswells, Wendover, Bkm
Bosworth Hall, Husbands Bosworth, Lei
Bottisham Hall, Bottisham, Cam
Boughton Hall, Boughton, Chs
Boughton House, Weekley, Nth
Boughton Mount, Boughton Monchelsea, Ken
Boughton Place, Boughton Malherbe, Ken
Boughton Place, Boughton Monchelsea, Ken
Boulge Hall, Boulge, Sfk
Bourn Hall, Bourn, Cam
Bourne Bank, Defford, Wor
Bourne Park, Bishopsbourne, Ken
Bournes, Wiveliscombe, Som
Bourton Hall, Bourton, War
Bourton House, Bourton, Brk
Bourton House, Bourton on the Hill, Gls
Bourton Manor, Much Wenlock, Sal
Bovacott, Bradford, Dev
Bowden Derra, Polyphant, Con
Bowden Hall, Chapel en le Frith, Dby
Bowden Hall, Upton St Leonards, Gls
Bowden Park, Bowden Hill, Wil
Bowdown House, Greenham, Brk
Bower House, Havering atte Bower, Ess
Bowers Wood, Nateby, Lan
Bownham House, Rodborough, Gls
Bowood, Bowood, Wil
Bowringsleigh, Alvington West, Dev
Bowscar, Penrith, Cul
Bowyers Court, Wisborough Green, Ssx
Boxted Hall, Boxted, Sfk
Boxwell Court, Boxwell with Leighterton, Gls
Boyce Court, Dymock, Gls
Boycott Manor House, Stowe, Bkm
Boyland Hall, Morningthorpe, Nfk
Boyles Court, South Weald, Ess
Boynes (The), Upton on Severn, Wor
Bozedown House, Whitchurch, Oxf
Brackenborough Hall, Brackenborough, Lin
Brackenborough Lawn, Brackenborough, Lin
Brackenburgh Tower, Plumpton Street, Cul
Brackenhurst Hall, Southwell, Ntt
Brackley House, Brackley, Nth
Bracon Hall, Bracon Ash, Nfk
Bradbourne, East Malling, Ken
Bradbourne Hall, Bradbourne, Dby
Bradden House, Bradden, Nth
Bradenham Hall, Bradenham, Nfk
Bradenham House, Bradenham, Bkm
Bradfield Hall, Bradfield, Brk
Bradfield Hall, Bradfield, Sfk
Bradfield, Uffculme, Dev
Bradford Peverell House, Bradford Peverell, Dor
Bradley Court, Chieveley, Brk
Bradley Hall, Bradley, Dby
Bradley Hall, Ryton, Dur

Bradley House, Maiden Bradley, Wil
Bradninch Manor, Bradninch, Dev
Bradridge House, Diptford, Dev
Bradwell Grove, Broadwell, Oxf
Brafferton Hall, Brafferton, Yks
Bragborough, Braunston, Nth
Bragbury End, Datchworth, Hrt
Brailsford Hall, Brailsford, Dby
Brainge (The), Putley, Hef
Bramall Hall, Bramhall, Chs
Bramall Hall, Stockport, Lan
Brambridge Park, Colden Common, Ham
Bramcote Hills, Bramcote, Ntt
Bramerton Grange, Bramerton, Nfk
Bramerton Hall, Bramerton, Nfk
Bramfield House, Bramfield, Sfk
Bramford Hall, Bramford, Sfk
Bramham Hall, Bramham cum Oglethorpe, Yks
Bramham Park, Bramham cum Oglethorpe, Yks
Bramlands, Woodmancote, Ssx
Bramley Park, Bramley, Sry
Brampton Bryan Hall, Brampton Bryan, Hef
Brampton Hall, Brampton, Sfk
Brampton House, Chapel Brampton, Nth
Brampton Manor, Brampton, Hun
Brampton Park, Brampton, Hun
Bramshill Park, Eversley, Ham
Brancepeth Castle, Brancepeth, Dur
Branches Park, Cowlinge, Sfk
Brand Hall, Norton in Hales, Sal
Brand (The), Woodhouse Eaves, Lei
Brandeston Hall, Brandeston, Sfk
Brandiston Hall, Brandiston, Nfk
Brandlingill, Blindbothel, Cul
Brandon Hall, Brandon, Sfk
Brandon Hall, Wolston, War
Brandon House, Brandon, Sfk
Brandon Park, Brandon, Sfk
Brandsby Hall, Brandsby, Yks
Brantham Court, Brantham, Sfk
Brantridge Park, Balcombe, Ssx
Brantwood, Coniston, Lan
Brasted Place, Brasted, Ken
Brathay Hall, Skelwith, Lan
Brattleby Hall, Brattleby, Lin
Braunstone Hall, Braunstone, Lei
Brawith Hall, Leake, Yks
Braxted Park, Great Braxted, Ess
Braydeston Hall, Bradeston, Nfk
Braye-du-Valle, St Sampson, Guernsey
Brayfield House, Cold Brayfield, Bkm
Braystones House, Braystones, Cul
Braywick House, Bray Wick, Brk
Braziers Park, Checkendon, Oxf
Breadsall Priory, Breadsall, Dby
Breakspears, Harefield, Mdx
Breamore House, Breamore, Ham
Breccles Hall, Breccles, Nfk
Breckenbrough Hall, Kirby Wiske, Yks
Bredfield House, Bredfield, Sfk

Brenley House, Boughton, Ken
Brent Knoll Manor House, Brent Knoll, Som
Brent Pelham Hall, Brent Pelham, Hrt
Brereton Hall, Brereton, Chs
Brettanby Manor, Barton, Yks
Brettenham Park, Brettenham, Sfk
Bretton Park, Bretton West, Yks
Brickendon Grange, Hertford, Hrt
Bricklehampton Hall, Bricklehampton, Wor
Brickworth House, Whiteparish, Wil
Bridehead, Littlebredy, Dor
Bridekirk, Bridekirk, Cul
Bridge House, South Petherton, Som
Bridwell, Halberton, Dev
Briery Close, Troutbeck, Wes
Briggens, Hunsdon, Hrt
Brightling Park, Brightling, Ssx
Brightwell Park, Brightwell Baldwin, Oxf
Brindle Lodge, Brindle, Lan
Brinkburn Priory, Brinkburn, Nbl
Brinkworth Hall, Elvington, Yks
Brinsop Court, Brinsop, Hef
Brixworth Hall, Brixworth, Nth
Broadclough Hall, Bacup, Lan
Broadfield Court, Bodenham, Hef
Broadfield House, Itonfield, Cul
Broadgate, Thwaites, Cul
Broadhanger, Froxfield, Ham
Broadhill, Keymer, Ssx
Broadlands, Romsey, Ham
Broadlands, Sunningdale, Brk
Broadlands, West Wratting, Sfk
Broadward Hall, Clungunford, Sal
Broadwell Hill, Broadwell, Gls
Brobury House, Brobury, Hef
Brocket Hall, Lemsford, Hrt
Brockfield Hall, Warthill, Yks
Brockhall Hall, Brockhall, Nth
Brockham Park, Betchworth, Sry
Brockham Warren, Betchworth, Sry
Brockhampton, Brockhampton near Bromyard, Hef
Brockhampton Court, Brockhampton near Ross, Hef
Brockhampton Park, Sevenhampton, Gls
Brockhill Park, Saltwood, Ken
Brocklesby Park, Brocklesby, Lin
Brockley Hall, Brockley, Som
Brocksford Hall, Doveridge, Dby
Brockwell Hall, Lambeth, Sry
Brockwood Park, Hinton Ampner, Ham
Brodsworth Hall, Brodsworth, Yks
Brogyntyn, Selattyn, Sal
Broke Hall, Nacton, Sfk
Brokenhurst Park, Brockenhurst, Ham
Brome Hall, Brome, Sfk
Bromesberrow Place, Bromesberrow, Gls
Bromham Hall, Bromham, Bdf
Bromhead Hall, Bolsterstone, Yks
Broncroft Castle, Diddlebury, Sal
Brook House, Highbrook, Ssx
Brooke Hall, Brooke, Nfk

Brooke House, Brook, Ham
Brooke House, Brooke, Nfk
Brooke House, Hackney, Mdx
Brookfield, Belbroughton, Wor
Brookfield Manor, Hathersage, Dby
Brookhill Hall, Pinxton, Dby
Brookhill, Kingswear, Dev
Brooklands, Swanwick, Ham
Brooksby Hall, Brooksby, Lei
Broom Hills, Botesdale, Sfk
Broom Leasoe, Whittington, Sts
Broome Hall, Capel, Sry
Broome Park, Barham, Ken
Broome Park, Betchworth, Sry
Broome Park, Edlingham, Nbl
Broome Place, Broome, Nfk
Broomford Manor, Jacobstowe, Dev
Broomham, Guestling, Ssx
Broomhill Bank, Speldhurst, Ken
Broomhill, Southborough, Ken
Broomhouse, Ancroft, Nbl
Broomsleigh, St Lawrence Seal, Ken
Broomy Close, Llanwarne, Hef
Brough Hall, Catterick, Yks
Brougham Hall, Brougham, Wes
Broughton Castle, Broughton, Oxf
Broughton Hall, Broughton, Yks
Broughton House, Broughton, Lan
Broughton House, Dunton Green, Ken
Broughton Lodge, Field Broughton, Lan
Broughton Tower, Broughton in Furness, Lan
Brownber, Newbiggin on Lune, Wes
Brownsea Castle, Brownsea Island, Dor
Brownsover Hall, Rugby, War
Browsholme Hall, Whitewell, Yks
Broxbornebury, Broxbourne, Hrt
Broxmore Park, Whiteparish, Wil
Broxton Lower Hall, Broxton, Chs
Broxton Old Hall, Broxton, Chs
Broxwood Court, Pembridge, Hef
Bruern Abbey, Milton under Wychwood, Oxf
Brushford Barton, Brushford, Dev
Brymore, Cannington, Som
Brympton House, Brympton, Som
Brynallt, Ellesmere, Sal
Brynderwen, Llanarth, Mon
Buckenham Tofts Hall, Buckenham Tofts, Nfk
Buckenhill House, Bromyard, Hef
Buckfield, Sherfield on Loddon, Ham
Buckhurst Park, Sunninghill, Brk
Buckhurst Park, Withyham, Ssx
Buckingham Palace, Westminster, Mdx
Buckland Abbey, Buckland Monachorum, Dev
Buckland Court, Buckland, Sry
Buckland House, Buckland, Brk
Buckland House, Buckland Filleigh, Dev
Buckland Manor, Buckland, Gls
Buckland Ripers Manor House, Buckland Ripers, Dor
Buckland Tout Saints, Buckland Tout Saints, Dev
Bucklebury Place, Bucklebury, Brk

Buckminster Park, Buckminster, Lei
Bucknell Manor, Bucknell, Oxf
Bude Castle, Bude, Con
Buglawton Hall, Buglawton, Chs
Buildwas Abbey, Buildwas, Sal
Buildwas Park, Buildwas, Sal
Bulby Hall, Irnham, Lin
Bulland Lodge, Chipstable, Som
Bullington Manor, Bullington, Ham
Bulstrode, Gerrard's Cross, Bkm
Bulwick Hall, Bulwick, Nth
Bunny Park, Bunny, Ntt
Burderop Park, Chisledon, Wil
Burdon Hall, Sunderland, Dur
Bure Homage, Christchurch, Ham
Burfield Hall, Wymondham, Nfk
Burford House, Burford, Sal
Burford Priory, Burford, Oxf
Burgate Manor, Fordingbridge, Ham
Burgh Hall, Burgh, Nfk
Burgh House, Burgh St Margaret, Nfk
Burgh House, Hampstead, Mdx
Burghclere Manor, Burghclere, Ham
Burghley House, Stamford, Lin
Burghley House, Stamford St Martin Baron, Nth
Burghwallis Hall, Burghwallis, Yks
Burkham House, Bentworth, Ham
Burleigh Court, Brimscombe, Gls
Burley Hall, Burley in Wharfedale, Yks
Burley House, Burley in Wharfedale, Yks
Burley Manor, Burley, Ham
Burley on the Hill, Burley, Rut
Burlton Hall, Loppington, Sal
Burlyns, East Woodhay, Ham
Burn Hall, Easingwold, Yks
Burncoose, Gwennap, Con
Burnham Priory, Burnham, Bkm
Burnhopeside Hall, Lanchester, Dur
Burnley Hall, East Somerton, Nfk
Burnt Norton, Weston sub Edge, Gls
Burrator House, Sheepstor, Dev
Burrow Hall, Tunstall, Lan
Burrs Wood, Old Groombridge, Ken
Burstone Manor, Zeal Monachorum, Dev
Burstow Hall, Burstow, Sry
Burton Agnes Hall, Burton Agnes, Yks
Burton Closes, Bakewell, Dby
Burton Court, Eardisland, Hef
Burton Hall, Burton by Lincoln, Lin
Burton Hall, Burton, Ham
Burton Hall, Burton on the Wolds, Lei
Burton Hill House, Malmesbury, Wil
Burton Lazars Hall, Burton Lazars, Lei
Burton Manor, Burton, Chs
Burton Park, Barlavington, Ssx
Burton Pynsent House, Curry Rivel, Som
Burtonfields Hall, East Stamford Bridge, Yks
Burwarton House, Burwarton, Sal
Burwell Park, Burwell, Lin
Burwood House, Walton on Thames, Sry

Bury Hill, Dorking, Sry
Bury (The), Pavenham, Bdf
Burythorpe House, Burythorpe, Yks
Busbridge Hall, Godalming, Sry
Busby Hall, Stokesley, Yks
Buscot Park, Buscot, Brk
Bushey House, Bushey, Hrt
Bushmead Priory, Eaton Socon, Bdf
Butcombe Court, Butcombe, Som
Butleigh Court, Butleigh, Som
Butler's Court, Beaconsfield, Bkm
Butley Hall, Butley, Chs
Butterley Hall, Ripley, Dby
Butterwick House, Hammersmith, Mdx
Buxhall Vale, Buxhall, Sfk
Buxshalls, Lindfield, Ssx
Buxted Park, Buxted, Ssx
Bydown, Swimbridge, Dev
Bylaugh Park, Bylaugh, Nfk
Byletts, Pembridge, Hef
Byrkley Lodge, Needwood Forest, Sts
Bystock, Withycombe Raleigh, Dev
Bywell Hall, Bywell, Nbl

Cadbury Court, North Cadbury, Som
Cadbury House, Congresbury, Som
Cadhay House, Ottery St Mary, Dev
Cadland House, Fareham, Ham
Caer-llan, Cwmcarvan, Mon
Caerhayes Castle, St Michael Caerhayes, Con
Caistor Hall, Caistor St Edmund, Nfk
Calder Abbey, Calderbridge, Cul
Caldicot Castle, Caldicot, Mon
Caldrees (The), Ickleton, Cam
Calehill, Little Chart, Ken
Calke Abbey, Calke, Dby
Callaly Castle, Callaly with Yetlington, Nbl
Callow Hall, Mappleton, Dby
Calthwaite Hall, Calthwaite, Cul
Calveley Hall, Calveley, Chs
Came House, Winterborne Came, Dor
Camer, Meopham, Ken
Camfield Place, Essendon, Hrt
Camp Hill, Burneston, Yks
Camp Hill Hall, Nuneaton, War
Campden House, Chipping Campden, Gls
Campsall Hall, Campsall, Yks
Campsmount, Campsall, Yks
Candlesby Hall, Candlesby, Lin
Cane End House, Kidmore End, Oxf
Cann House, Tanerton Foliot, Dev
Cannon Hall, Cawthorne, Yks
Cannon Hall, Hampstead, Mdx
Canon Frome Court, Canon Frome, Hef
Canonbury House, Islington, Mdx
Canons Ashby, Canons Ashby, Nth
Canonsgrove, Pitminster, Som
Canonteign House, Christow, Dev
Canterton Manor, Minstead, Ham
Cantley Hall, Cantley, Yks

INDEX OF ENGLISH COUNTRY HOUSES

Canwick Hall, Canwick, Lin
Capel House, Enfield, Mdx
Capel Leyse, Capel, Sry
Capel Manor, Horsmonden, Ken
Capenhurst Hall, Capenhurst, Chs
Capernwray Hall, Over Kellet, Lan
Capesthorne Hall, Capesthorne, Chs
Capheaton Hall, Kirkwhelpington, Nbl
Car Colston Hall, Car Colston, Ntt
Caradoc Court, Sellack, Hef
Carelew, Mylor, Con
Careys, Brockenhurst, Ham
Carleton Hall, Carleton Cowper, Cul
Carleton Hall, Carleton, Cul
Carlton Curlieu Hall, Carlton Curlieu, Lei
Carlton Hall, Carlton in Lindrick, Ntt
Carlton Hall, Carlton on Trent, Ntt
Carlton Hall, Kelsale, Sfk
Carlton Manor House, Guiseley, Yks
Carlton Scroop Hall, Carlton Scroop, Lin
Carlton Towers, Carlton near Snaith, Yks
Carnanton, Mawgan in Pydar, Con
Carnfield Hall, South Normanton, Dby
Carrow Abbey, Norwich, Nfk
Carrycoats Hall, Thockrington, Nbl
Carswell Manor, Buckland, Brk
Carus Lodge, Halton with Aughton, Lan
Casewick Hall, Uffington, Lin
Cassia Lodge, Marton, Chs
Casterton Hall, Casterton, Wes
Casterton Old Hall, Casterton, Wes
Castle Ashby, Castle Ashby, Nth
Castle Combe Manor House, Castle Combe, Wil
Castle Goring, Worthing, Ssx
Castle Hill, Filleigh, Dev
Castle Horneck, Madron, Con
Castle House, Usk, Mon
Castle Howard, Castle Howard, Yks
Castle, Lanlivery Rural, Con
Castle Malwood, Minstead, Ham
Castle Park, Frodsham, Chs
Castle Rising Hall, Castle Rising, Nfk
Castle (The), Castle Eden, Dur
Castle (The), St Michael's Mount, Con
Castle, Wiveliscombe, Som
Castlesteads, Low Walton, Cul
Castletown House, Rockcliffe, Cul
Catchfrench, Hessenford, Con
Catesby House, Catesby, Nth
Catfield Hall, Catfield, Nfk
Catherston House, Catherston Leweston, Dor
Caton Hall, Caton, Lan
Catthorpe Manor, Catthorpe, Lei
Catton Hall, Catton, Nfk
Catton Hall, Croxall, Sts
Catton House, Catton, Nfk
Caundle Purse Manor House, Caundle Purse, Dor
Cave Castle, South Cave, Yks
Cavenham Park, Cavenham, Sfk
Caversfield House, Caversfield, Oxf

Caves (The), Banwell, Som
Cawston Manor House, Cawston, Nfk
Caynham Court, Caynham, Sal
Caythorpe Court, Caythorpe, Lin
Caythorpe Hall, Caythorpe, Lin
Cayton Hall, South Stainley with Cayton, Yks
Cefntilla Court, Llandenny, Mon
Chacombe House, Chacombe, Nth
Chacombe Priory, Chacombe, Nth
Chaddlewood, Plympton St Mary, Dev
Chaffcombe House, Chaffcombe, Som
Chagford House, Chagford, Dev
Chalcot, Dilton Marsh, Wil
Chalmington House, Cattistock, Dor
Champion Lodge, Great Totham, Ess
Chanter's House (The), Ottery St Mary, Dev
Chantmarle, Cattistock, Dor
Chantry House, Turvey, Bdf
Chantry (The), Bradford on Avon, Wil
Chantry (The), Chantry, Som
Chantry (The), Sproughton, Sfk
Chapel Cleeve, Old Cleeve, Som
Chapelwood Manor, Nutley, Ssx
Chappels, Thwaites, Cul
Charborough Park, Morden, Dor
Chargot, Luxborough, Som
Charlecote Park, Charlecote, War
Charley Hall, Charley, Lei
Charlton Hall, Ellingham, Nbl
Charlton House, Charlton, Ken
Charlton House, Hartlebury, Wor
Charlton House, Shepton Mallet, Som
Charlton Lodge, Newbottle, Nth
Charlton Mackrell Court, Charlton Mackrell, Som
Charlton Manor, Charlton, Wor
Charlton Musgrove, Charlton Musgrove, Som
Charlton Park, Charlton Kings, Gls
Charlton Park, Charlton, Wil
Charlton Place, Bishopsbourne, Ken
Charlwood Park, Charlwood, Sry
Charnes Hall, Croxton, Sts
Charnwood Lodge, Charley, Lei
Charterhouse, Charterhouse, Mdx
Charters, Sunningdale, Brk
Chartham Park, Lingfield, Sry
Chartridge Lodge, Chartridge, Bkm
Chase Cliffe, Crich, Dby
Chastleton House, Chastleton, Oxf
Chatley, Woolverton, Som
Chatsworth House, Chatsworth, Dby
Chattan, Axminster, Dev
Chavenage, Horsley, Gls
Chawton House, Chawton, Ham
Checkendon Court, Checkendon, Oxf
Chedington Court, Chedington, Dor
Chediston Hall, Chediston, Sfk
Cheeseburn Grange, Stamfordham, Nbl
Chelwood Beacon, Nutley, Ssx
Chelwood Vetchery, Nutley, Ssx
Chenies House, Chenies, Bkm

Chequers, Ellesborough, Bkm
Cherington Park, Cherington, Gls
Cherkley Court, Leatherhead, Sry
Cherry Burton Hall, Cherry Burton, Yks
Cherry Burton House, Cherry Burton, Yks
Chesfield Park, Graveley, Hrt
Chesham Bois Manor, Chesham Bois, Bkm
Chesham Bury, Chesham, Bkm
Cheshunt Park, Cheshunt, Hrt
Chestal, Dursley, Gls
Chesterfield House, Greenwich, Ken
Chesterford Park, Little Chesterford, Ess
Chesters, Warden, Nbl
Chesterton Lodge, Chesterton, Oxf
Chestham Park, Henfield, Ssx
Chestnut Grove Hall, Boston Spa, Yks
Chestnut Lodge, Hampstead, Mdx
Cheswardine Hall, Cheswardine, Sal
Cheswick House, Ancroft, Nbl
Chettle House, Chettle, Dor
Chetwode Manor, Chetwode, Bkm
Chetwynd Park, Cheswardine Rural, Sal
Chevening Place, Chevening, Ken
Chevet Hall, Chevet, Yks
Chevithorne Barton, Tiverton, Dev
Chew Court, Chew Magna, Som
Chew Magna Manor House, Chew Magna, Som
Chewton Priory, Chewton Mendip, Som
Chicheley Hall, Chicheley, Bkm
Chichester Palace, Chichester, Ssx
Chicksands Priory, Chicksands, Bdf
Chiddingstone Castle, Chiddingstone, Ken
Chideock Manor House, Chideock, Dor
Child Okeford Manor, Child Okeford, Dor
Childerley Hall, Childerley, Cam
Childown Hall, Chertsey, Sry
Childrey Manor House, Childrey, Brk
Childs Ercall Hall, Childs Ercall, Sal
Childwick Bury, St Albans, Hrt
Chilham Castle, Chilham, Ken
Chillingham Castle, Chillingham, Nbl
Chillington Hall, Brewood, Sts
Chilston Park, Boughton Malherbe, Ken
Chilton Cantelo, Chilton Cantelo, Som
Chilton House, Chilton, Bkm
Chilton, Hungerford, Brk
Chilworth Manor, Chilworth, Ham
Chilworthy House, Ilminster, Som
Chipchase Castle, Chollerton, Nbl
Chipley Park, Nynehead, Som
Chippenham Park, Chippenham, Cam
Chithurst House, Chithurst, Ssx
Chittlehamholt Manor, Chittlehamholt, Dev
Chobham Place, Chobham, Sry
Cholderton Lodge, Amport, Ham
Cholmondeley Castle, Cholmondeley, Chs
Chorlton Hall, Chorlton by Backford, Chs
Chorlton Hall, Chorlton, Chs
Christleton Hall, Christleton, Chs
Church Beck House, Scalby, Yks

Churchdale Hall, Ashford, Dby
Churston Manor, West Putford, Dev
Chute Lodge, Chute Forest, Wil
Chyanhall, Gulval, Con
Chyverton, Perranzabuloe, Con
Cirencester Abbey, Cirencester, Gls
Cirencester House, Cirencester, Gls
Clandon Park, West Clandon, Sry
Clanna, Alvington, Gls
Clanville Lodge, Weyhill, Ham
Clanville, Minehead, Som
Clapham Park, Clapham, Bdf
Clare Hall, Ston Easton, Som
Clare Priory, Clare, Sfk
Clarence House, St James Westminster, Mdx
Clarendon Park, Clarendon Park, Wil
Clatford Mills, Upper Clatford, Ham
Claughton Hall, Claughton on Brock, Lan
Claverdon Leys, Claverdon, War
Claverton Manor House, Claverton, Som
Claybrooke Hall, Claybrooke, Lei
Claydon House, Lechlade, Gls
Claydon House, Middle Claydon, Bkm
Claydon Old Hall, Claydon, Sfk
Clayton Hall, Clayton le Moors, Lan
Clayton Hall, Newcastle under Lyme, Sts
Clayton Priory, Clayton, Ssx
Clayworth Hall, Clayworth, Ntt
Clearwell Castle, Clearwell, Gls
Cleeve Grange, Bishop's Cleeve, Gls
Cleeve House, Bishop's Cleeve, Gls
Cleeve House, Seend, Wil
Cleeve (The), Rodbourne, Wil
Cleobury Court, Cleobury North, Sal
Clerk Hill, Whalley, Lan
Clervaux Castle, Croft, Yks
Clevedon Court, Clevedon, Som
Clevedon Hall, Clevedon, Som
Clewer Park, Clewer, Brk
Cliff Park Hall, Horton, Sts
Cliff (The), Terrington, Yks
Cliffe Castle, Keighley, Yks
Cliffe Hall, Manfield, Yks
Clifford Manor, Cliffords Mesne, Gls
Clifton Castle, Thornton Watlass, Yks
Clifton Hall, Clifton with Glapton, Ntt
Clifton Hall, Lund, Lan
Clifton Hill, Forton, Lan
Clippesby Hall, Clippesby, Nfk
Clipsham Hall, Clipsham, Rut
Clissold House, Stoke Newington, Mdx
Clive Hall, Clive, Sal
Cliveden, Taplow, Bkm
Clopton Hall, Rattlesden, Sfk
Close House, Wylam, Nbl
Clouds House, East Knoyle, Wil
Clovelly Court, Clovelly, Dev
Clowance, Crowan, Con
Clumber Park, Worksop, Ntt
Clyffe, Tincleton, Dor

INDEX OF ENGLISH COUNTRY HOUSES

Clytha Park, Llanarth, Mon
Coates House, Coates, Ssx
Coates Manor, Coates, Gls
Cobham Hall, Cobham, Ken
Cobham Park, Cobham, Sry
Cockermouth Castle, Cockermouth, Cul
Cockfield Hall, Yoxford, Sfk
Cockley Cley Hall, Cockley Cley, Nfk
Coddington Court, Coddington, Hef
Codicote Lodge, Codicote, Hrt
Cofyns, Spreyton, Dev
Coghurst Hall, Ore, Ssx
Cogshall Hall, Cogshall, Chs
Coham, Black Torrington, Dev
Cokenach, Barkway, Hrt
Coker Court, East Coker, Som
Cokethorpe Park, Ducklington, Oxf
Cold Overton Hall, Cold Overton, Lei
Coldbrook Park, Abergavenny, Mon
Coldham Hall, Stanningfield, Sfk
Coldharbour Wood, Milland, Ssx
Coldhayes, Steep, Ham
Coldrenick, Menheniot, Con
Cole Park, Malmesbury, Wil
Coleby Hall, Coleby, Lin
Colehays, Bovey Tracey, Dev
Coleorton Hall, Coleorton, Lei
Coles Park, Westmill, Hrt
Colesborne Park, Colesborne, Gls
Coleshill House, Coleshill, Brk
Colinshayes Manor, Brewham, Som
College of Arms, St Benet Paul's Wharf, Lnd
College (The), Kirkoswald, Cul
Colleton Manor, Chulmleigh, Dev
Collipriest House, Tiverton, Dev
Coln St Aldwyns Manor House, Coln St Aldwyns, Gls
Colne Ford House, Earls Colne, Ess
Colne House, Earls Colne, Ess
Colne Park, Colne Engaine, Ess
Colney Hall, Colney, Nfk
Colquite, St Mabyn, Con
Colston Hall, Colston Bassett, Ntt
Coltishall House, Coltishall, Nfk
Coltishall Mead, Coltishall, Nfk
Coly House, Colyford, Dev
Comarques, Thorpe le Soken, Ess
Combe Abbey, Combe Fields, War
Combe Court, Chiddingfold, Sry
Combe Florey House, Combe Florey, Som
Combe, Gittisham, Dev
Combe Hay Manor, Combe Hay, Som
Combe House, Combe, Hef
Combe Sydenham, Stogumber, Som
Combehead, Bampton, Dev
Combermere Abbey, Dodcott cum Wilksley, Chs
Compton Castle, Compton Pauncefoot, Som
Compton Durville Manor, South Petherton, Som
Compton House, Compton Beauchamp, Brk
Compton House, Over Compton, Dor
Compton Manor, King's Somborne, Ham

Compton Park, Compton Chamberlayne, Wil
Compton Place, Eastbourne, Ssx
Compton Regis House, Compton Beauchamp, Brk
Compton Verney House, Compton Verney, War
Compton Wynyates House, Compton Wynyates, War
Condover Hall, Condover, Sal
Coney Weston Hall, Coney Weston, Sfk
Congham Hall, Congham, Nfk
Congham House, Congham, Nfk
Congham Lodge, Congham, Nfk
Conholt Park, Chute, Wil
Conigree Court, Newent, Gls
Conington Castle, Conington, Hun
Conington Hall, Conington, Cam
Coniston Hall, Coniston Cold, Yks
Consall Hall, Wetley Rocks, Sts
Constable Burton Hall, Fingall, Yks
Conyboro, Barcombe, Ssx
Conyngham Hall, Knaresborough, Yks
Coolhurst, Horsham, Ssx
Coombe House, Donhead St Mary, Wil
Coombe Lodge, Blagdon, Som
Coombe Park, Whitchurch, Oxf
Coombe Place, Hamsey, Ssx
Coombe Trenchard, Lew Trenchard, Dev
Copgrove Hall, Copgrove, Yks
Cople House, Cople, Bdf
Coplow (The), Billesdon, Lei
Copped Hall, Epping Upland, Ess
Coppice (The), Shiplake, Oxf
Copplestone House, Copplestone, Dev
Copsale Court, Nuthurst, Ssx
Copse Hill, Upper Slaughter, Gls
Copt Hewick Hall, Copt Hewick, Yks
Coptfold Hall, Margaretting, Ess
Corby Castle, Holme Eden, Cul
Corfton Hall, Diddlebury, Sal
Corhampton House, Corhampton, Ham
Cornborough, Abbotsham, Dev
Cornbury Park, Cornbury Park, Oxf
Cornhill House, Cornhill, Nbl
Cornhill, Pattishall, Nth
Cornwell Manor, Cornwell, Oxf
Corsham Court, Corsham, Wil
Coryton Park, Kilmington, Dev
Cosgrove Hall, Cosgrove, Nth
Cosgrove Priory, Cosgrove, Nth
Cossington Manor, Cossington, Som
Cote House, Aston, Oxf
Cotefield House, Adderbury, Oxf
Cotehele House, Calstock, Con
Cotesbach Hall, Cotesbach, Lei
Cotgrave Place, Cotgrave, Ntt
Cothelstone House, Cothelston, Som
Cotheridge Court, Cotheridge, Wor
Cotmore House, Fringford, Oxf
Coton Hall, Alveley, Sal
Coton Hall, Edstaston, Sal
Coton Hall, Hanbury, Sts
Coton House, Churchover, War

11

INDEX OF ENGLISH COUNTRY HOUSES

Cotswold Park, North Cerney, Gls
Cotterstock Hall, Cotterstock, Nth
Cottesbrooke Hall, Cottesbrooke, Nth
Cottles Park, Atworth, Wil
Coughton Court, Coughton, War
Cound Hall, Cound, Sal
Coupland Castle, Kirknewton, Nbl
Court Barton, Exbourne, Dev
Court Hall, North Molton, Dev
Court House, East Quantoxhead, Som
Court House, Nether Stowey, Som
Court House (The), Painswick, Gls
Court Lodge, Lamberhurst, Ken
Court Moor, Crookham, Ham
Court of Hill, Burford, Sal
Court Place, Bathealton, Som
Court Place, Iffley, Oxf
Court (The), Chetnole, Dor
Courteenhall House, Courteenhall, Nth
Courtfield, Welsh Bicknor, Hef
Courthouse (The), Birlingham, Wor
Coventry Hall, Streatham, Sry
Cowarne Court, Much Cowarne, Hef
Cowdray Park, Easebourne, Ssx
Cowesby Hall, Cowesby, Yks
Cowesfield House, Whiteparish, Wil
Cowley Manor, Cowley, Gls
Cowling Hall, Bedale, Yks
Coworth Park, Sunningdale, Brk
Coxhoe Hall, Coxhoe, Dur
Crabbet Park, Worth, Ssx
Crackenthorpe Hall, Crackenthorpe, Wes
Craddock House, Uffculme, Dev
Craggs (The), Broughton, Cul
Cragside, Morpeth, Nbl
Crakehall Hall, Great Crakehall, Yks
Crakemarsh Hall, Crakemarsh, Sts
Cranage Hall, Cranage, Chs
Cranborne Manor House, Cranborne, Dor
Cranbury Park, Hursley, Ham
Cranesden, Mayfield, Ssx
Cranford Hall, Cranford St Andrew, Nth
Cranley Grange, Eye, Sfk
Cranmer Hall, Sculthorpe, Nfk
Cranmore Hall, East Cranmore, Som
Cransford Hall, Cransford, Sfk
Cransley Hall, Cransley, Nth
Craster Tower, Embleton, Nbl
Crathorne Hall, Crathorne, Yks
Crawley Court, Crawley, Ham
Crawley Grange, North Crawley, Bkm
Crawshaw Hall, Rawtenstall, Lan
Craycombe House, Fladbury, Wor
Crayke Castle, Crayke, Yks
Craythorne, Rolleston, Sts
Creech Grange, Steeple, Dor
Creedy Park, Sandford, Dev
Creskeld Hall, Arthington, Yks
Cresswell Hall, Cresswell, Nbl
Crewe Hall, Crewe Green, Chs

Crewe Hill, Crewe, Chs
Crichel House, More Crichel, Dor
Cricket Court, Cricket Malherbie, Som
Cricket House, Cricket St Thomas, Som
Crickleaze, Combe St Nicholas, Som
Crippenden Manor, Cowden, Ken
Crix, Hatfield Peverel, Ess
Croft Castle, Croft, Hef
Croft House, Somerford Keynes, Gls
Croft (The), Kirksanton, Cul
Croft-y-Bwla, Monmouth, Mon
Crofton Hall, Crofton, Cul
Crofton Hall, Crofton, Yks
Cromer Hall, Cromer, Nfk
Cromwell House, Highgate, Mdx
Crookham House, Crookham, Ham
Crookham House, Thatcham, Brk
Crookhey, Cockerham, Lan
Croome Court, Croome D'Abitot, Wor
Crosby Court, North Otterington, Yks
Crosby Hall, Little Crosby, Lan
Crosby House, High Crosby, Cul
Crosby Lodge, High Crosby, Cul
Croslands, Barrow in Furness, Lan
Cross House, Bootle, Cul
Crossrigg Hall, Bolton, Wes
Croughton House, Croughton, Nth
Crowborough Warren, Withyham St John, Ssx
Crowcombe Court, Crowcombe, Som
Crowdleham House, Kemsing, Ken
Crowe Hall, Stutton, Sfk
Crowham Manor, Westfield, Ssx
Crowhurst Park, Crowhurst, Ssx
Crowhurst Place, Crowhurst, Sry
Crown Point House, Trowse Newton, Nfk
Crowsley Park, Shiplake, Oxf
Croxall Hall, Croxall, Sts
Croxdale Hall, Croxdale, Dur
Croxteth Hall, Croxteth Park, Lan
Croxton Park, Croxton, Cam
Cruckton Hall, Pontesbury, Sal
Cruwys Morchard House, Cruwys Morchard, Dev
Cuckfield Park, Cuckfield, Ssx
Cuddesdon Palace, Cuddesdon, Oxf
Cuerden Hall, Bamber Bridge, Lan
Cuffnells, Lyndhurst, Ham
Culcheth Hall, Newchurch Kenyon, Lan
Culford Hall, Culford, Sfk
Culham Court, Upper Culham, Brk
Culmhead, Pitminster, Som
Culmington Manor, Culmington, Sal
Culver House, Holcombe Burnell, Dev
Culver House (The), Amberley, Gls
Culverlands, Burghfield, Brk
Culverthorpe Hall, Heydour, Lin
Culverwood House, Little Berkhamsted, Hrt
Cumberland Lodge, Old Windsor, Brk
Cundall Manor, Cundall, Yks
Cupola (The), Leiston, Sfk
Curwen Woods, Holme, Wes

Cusworth Hall, Sprotborough, Yks
Cuxwold Hall, Cuxwold, Lin

Dagnam Park, Noak Hill, Ess
Dalby Hall, Dalby, Lin
Dalby Hall, Little Dalby, Lei
Dale Park, Madehurst, Ssx
Dale (The), Moston, Chs
Daleford, Marton, Chs
Dalemain, Dacre, Cul
Dalham Hall, Dalham, Sfk
Dalicott House, Claverley, Sal
Dallam Tower, Haverbrack, Wes
Dalston Hall, Buckabank, Cul
Dalton Hall, Carnforth, Lan
Dalton Hall, Dalton Holme, Yks
Dalton Hall, Dalton, Wes
Danbury Park, Danbury, Ess
Danby Hall, Thornton Steward, Yks
Danby Lodge, Danby, Yks
Dane Court, Tilmanstone, Ken
Danehurst, Danehill, Ssx
Danemore Park, Speldhurst, Ken
Danesbury, Welwyn, Hrt
Danesfield, Medmenham, Bkm
Danny, Hurstpierpoint, Ssx
Darenth Grange, Darenth, Ken
Daresbury Hall, Daresbury, Chs
Darlaston Hall, Darlaston, Sts
Darley Dale Hall, Darley Dale, Dby
Darnhall Hall, Darnhall, Chs
Darsham House, Darsham, Sfk
Dartington Hall, Dartington, Dev
Darwen Bank, Walton le Dale, Lan
Dauntsey Park, Dauntsey, Wil
Davenham Hall, Davenham, Chs
Davenport, Worfield, Sal
Davenshaw House, Buglawton, Chs
Dawnedge, Aspley Guise, Bdf
Deal Castle, Deal, Ken
Dean Hall, Little Dean, Gls
Dean's Court, Wimborne, Dor
Deane House, Deane, Ham
Debdale Hall, Mansfield Woodhouse, Ntt
Decker Hill, Shifnal, Sal
Deene Park, Deene, Nth
Deer Park, Buckerell, Dev
Deighton Grove, Naburn, Yks
Deighton Manor House, Northallerton, Yks
Delamere House, Cuddington, Chs
Delamore, Cornwood, Dev
Delapré Abbey, Hardingstone, Nth
Delbury Hall, Diddlebury, Sal
Denbies, Dorking, Sry
Denbury Manor, Denbury, Dev
Denby Grange, Upper Whitley, Yks
Dene Park, Hadlow, Ken
Denham Court, Denham, Bkm
Denham Place, Denham, Bkm
Denne Hill, Womenswould, Ken

Denne Park, Horsham, Ssx
Dennington House, Swimbridge, Dev
Denston Hall, Denston, Sfk
Denton Court, Denton, Ken
Denton Hall, Newcastle, Nbl
Denton House, Denton, Nfk
Denton Lodge, Denton, Nfk
Denton Manor, Denton, Lin
Denton Park, Denton, Yks
Depper Hall, Hoxne, Sfk
Derby House (College of Arms), St Benet
  Paul's Wharf, Lnd
Derriads, Chippenham, Wil
Derriford, Egg Buckland, Dev
Derry's Wood, Wonersh, Sry
Dersingham Hall, Dersingham, Nfk
Derwent Hill, Crosthwaite, Cul
Devereux House, Coleshill, War
Devizes Castle, Devizes, Wil
Dewlish House, Dewlish, Dor
Dicker (The), Hellingly, Ssx
Diddington Hall, Diddington, Hun
Didlington Hall, Didlington, Nfk
Dieulacres Abbey, Leek, Sts
Dillington Park, Ilminster, Som
Dilston, Corbridge, Nbl
Dilworth House, Longridge, Lan
Dinder House, Dinder, Som
Dingestow Court, Dingestow, Mon
Dingley Hall, Dingley, Nth
Dinmore Manor House, Dinmore, Hef
Dinnington Hall, Dinnington, Yks
Dinorben Court, Crookham, Ham
Dinton Hall, Dinton, Bkm
Dinton House, Dinton, Wil
Dipton House, Riding Mill, Nbl
Dissington Hall, Newcastle, Nbl
Ditcham Park, Buriton, Ham
Ditcheat Priory, Ditcheat, Som
Ditchingham Hall, Ditchingham, Nfk
Ditchley Park, Spelsbury, Oxf
Ditton Place, Staplefield, Ssx
Dixton Manor, Alderton, Gls
Dobroyd Castle, Todmorden, Lan
Docking Hall, Docking, Nfk
Doddershall Park, Quainton, Bkm
Doddington Hall, Doddington, Chs
Doddington Hall, Doddington, Lin
Dodington House, Dodington, Gls
Dodworth Hall, Dodworth, Yks
Dogmersfield Park, Dogmersfield, Ham
Dole, Hurstbourne Tarrant, Ham
Donhead Hall, Donhead St Mary, Wil
Donhead House, Donhead St Andrew, Wil
Donnington Castle House, Shaw, Brk
Donnington Grove, Shaw, Brk
Donnington Hall, Donnington, Hef
Dorfold Hall, Acton, Chs
Dorney Court, Dorney, Bkm
Dorton House, Dorton, Bkm

Doublebois House, Liskeard, Con
Douglas House, Petersham, Sry
Douthwaite Dale, Lastingham, Yks
Dove Leys, Denstone, Sts
Dovenby Hall, Dovenby, Cul
Doveridge Hall, Doveridge, Dby
Dowdeswell Court, Dowdeswell, Gls
Dower House, Canwick, Lin
Dower House, Ewerby, Lin
Down House, Blandford St Mary, Dor
Down House, Shapwick, Som
Down Place, Compton, Sry
Downes, Crediton, Dev
Downlands, Bramshott, Ham
Downs House, East Hendred, Brk
Downs House, Yalding, Ken
Downshire House, Putney, Sry
Downton Castle, Downton, Hef
Downton Hall, Stanton Lacy, Sal
Dowsby Hall, Dowsby, Lin
Doxford Hall, Ellingham, Nbl
Drax Hall, Drax, Yks
Draycot House, Draycot, Wil
Draycott Hall, Reeth, Yks
Draycott House, Draycott, Dby
Drayton Hall, Drayton, Nfk
Drayton Hall, West Drayton, Mdx
Drayton House, Lowick, Nth
Drayton Park, Barton Stacey, Ham
Drinkstone Park, Drinkstone, Sfk
Dropmore, Dropmore, Bkm
Dryderdale Hall, South Bedburn, Dur
Duddon Hall, Duddon Bridge, Cul
Dudmaston, Quatt, Sal
Dudwick House, Buxton, Nfk
Dullingham House, Dullingham, Cam
Dumbleton Hall, Dumbleton, Gls
Dummer House, Dummer, Ham
Dunchideock House, Dunchideock, Dev
Dundridge, Harberton, Dev
Dunham Lodge, Little Dunham, Nfk
Dunkenhalgh, Clayton le Moors, Lan
Dunmore, Bradninch, Dev
Dunningwell, The Green, Cul
Dunsland Court, Jacobstowe, Dev
Dunsland Manor, Bradford, Dev
Dunstall Court, Fakenham, Wor
Dunstall Hall, Dunstall, Sts
Dunstall Priory, Shoreham, Ken
Dunster Castle, Dunster, Som
Dunston Hall, Dunston, Nfk
Duntish Court, Buckland Newton, Dor
Dunton Bassett Manor House, Dunton Bassett, Lei
Dunwood Manor, Awbridge, Ham
Durdans (The), Epsom, Sry
Durnford Manor House, Durnford, Wil
Duxbury Hall, Adlington, Lan
Dynes Hall, Great Maplestead, Ess
Dyrham Park, Dyrham, Gls
Dyrham Park, South Mimms, Mdx

Eagle House, Eltham, Ken
Eagle House, Hackney, Mdx
Earlham Hall, Earlham, Nfk
Earlsdale, Pontesbury, Sal
Earnshill, Hambridge, Som
Earsham Hall, Earsham, Nfk
Eartham House, Eartham, Ssx
Easby Hall, Ayton, Yks
Eashing Park, Godalming, Sry
Easneye, Stanstead Abbotts, Hrt
East Barsham Manor, East Barsham, Nfk
East Bergholt Place, East Bergholt, Sfk
East Bilney Hall, East Bilney, Nfk
East Carleton Lodge, East Carleton, Nfk
East Carleton Manor House, East Carleton, Nfk
East Court, East Grinstead, Ssx
East Court, Wookey, Som
East Cowes Castle, East Cowes, Ham
East Farleigh Priory, East Farleigh, Ken
East Haddon Hall, East Haddon, Nth
East Hall, Feltwell, Nfk
East Hall, Middleton Tyas, Yks
East Layton Hall, Forcett, Yks
East Lodge, Rolleston, Sts
East Norton Hall, East Norton, Lei
East Sutton Park, East Sutton, Ken
East Winch Hall, East Winch, Nfk
Eastbridge, Crondall, Ham
Eastbury Manor, Compton, Sry
Eastbury Park, Tarrant Gunville, Dor
Eastcliff, Bembridge, Ham
Eastcourt House, Crudwell, Wil
Eastcroft, Harrington, Cul
Eastham Grange, Eastham, Wor
Easthampstead Park, Easthampstead, Brk
Easthill, Rodden, Som
Easthorpe Hall, Appleton le Street, Yks
Eastington Hall, Longdon, Wor
Eastington House, Ampney St Peter, Gls
Eastington House, Stonehouse, Gls
Eastington Park, Stonehouse, Gls
Eastleigh, Bishopstrow, Wil
Eastnor Castle, Eastnor, Hef
Eastoft Hall, Eastoft, Lin
Eastoft Hall, Eastoft, Yks
Easton Court, Little Hereford, Hef
Easton Hall, Stoke Rochford, Lin
Easton Lodge, Little Easton, Ess
Easton Neston House, Easton Neston, Nth
Eastwell Park, Eastwell, Ken
Eastwood Park, Falfield, Gls
Eathorpe Park, Wappenbury, War
Eaton Grange, Eaton, Lei
Eaton Hall, Eaton, Chs
Eaton Hall, Eaton, Ntt
Eaton Hall, Eccleston, Chs
Eaves Hall, Waddington, Yks
Ebberly House, Roborough, Dev
Ebworth Park, Sheepscombe, Gls
Eccle Riggs, Broughton in Furness, Lan

INDEX OF ENGLISH COUNTRY HOUSES

Eccles Hall, Eccles, Nfk
Eccles House, Chapel en le Frith, Dby
Eccleshall Castle, Eccleshall, Sts
Eckington Hall, Eckington, Dby
Ecton Hall, Ecton, Nth
Eden Grove, Bolton, Wes
Eden Grove, Low Crosby, Cul
Eden Hall, Mark Beech, Ken
Eden Lacy, Great Salkeld, Cul
Eden Place, Hartley, Wes
Edgarley Hall, Glastonbury, Som
Edgcote House, Edgcote, Nth
Edge Barton Manor, Branscombe, Dev
Edge Hall, Edge, Chs
Edgeworth Manor, Edgeworth, Gls
Edith Weston Hall, Edith Weston, Rut
Edmond Castle, Hayton, Cul
Edmondsham Manor House, Edmondsham, Dor
Edmondthorpe Hall, Edmondthorpe, Lei
Ednaston Lodge, Brailsford, Dby
Edstaston House, Edstaston, Sal
Edwardstone Hall, Edwardstone, Sfk
Efford Park, Milford on Sea, Ham
Egginton Hall, Egginton, Dby
Egglestone Hall, Egglestone, Dur
Eglingham Hall, Eglingham, Nbl
Egton Manor, Egton, Yks
Elcot Park, Kintbury, Brk
Elemore Hall, Durham, Dur
Elkington Hall, South Elkington, Lin
Ellel Grange, Ellel, Lan
Ellen Bank, Birkby, Cul
Ellenside House, Ireby, Cul
Ellergreen, Strickland Ketel, Wes
Ellerton Hall, Cheswardine, Sal
Ellingham Hall, Ellingham, Nbl
Ellingham Hall, Ellingham, Nfk
Ellingham Hall, Little Ellingham, Nfk
Elm House, Castle Bolton, Yks
Elm Lodge, Ravenstonedale, Wes
Elmbridge Court, Hucclecote, Gls
Elmdon Bury, Elmdon, Ess
Elmestree, Tetbury Upton, Gls
Elmley Castle, Elmley Castle, Wor
Elmore Court, Elmore, Gls
Elms (The), Acton Grange, Chs
Elms (The), Houghton, Hun
Elmstone Court, Elmstone, Ken
Elsham Hall, Elsham, Lin
Elston Hall, Elston, Ntt
Elterwater Hall, Great and Little Langdale, Wes
Eltham Lodge, Eltham, Ken
Eltham Palace, Eltham, Ken
Elton Hall, Elton, Dur
Elton Hall, Elton, Hun
Elton Manor, Elton, Ntt
Elvaston Castle, Elvaston, Dby
Elveden Hall, Elveden, Sfk
Elvetham Hall, Elvetham, Ham
Ely Grange, Frant, Ssx

Ely Palace, Ely, Cam
Ely Place, Holborn, Mdx
Embley Park, East Wellow, Ham
Encombe, Kingston, Dor
Enderby Hall, Enderby, Lei
Endsleigh Cottage, Milton Abbot, Dev
Enfield House, Hampstead, Mdx
Englefield House, Englefield, Brk
Englemere, Ascot, Brk
Enmore Castle, Enmore, Som
Ennim, Great Blencow, Cul
Enville Hall, Enville, Sts
Enys, St Gluvias, Con
Epperstone Manor, Epperstone, Ntt
Epping House, Little Berkhamsted, Hrt
Eridge Castle, Eridge Green, Ssx
Erlegh Park, Earley, Brk
Erskine House, Hampstead, Mdx
Erway, Dudleston, Sal
Erwood Hall, Taxal, Chs
Escot, Escot, Dev
Escowbeck, Quernmore, Lan
Eshott Hall, Felton, Nbl
Eshton Hall, Gargrave, Yks
Esk Hall, Eskdaleside cum Ugglebarnby, Yks
Eskmeals House, Eskmeals, Cul
Eslington Park, Eslington, Nbl
Espley Hall, Mitford, Nbl
Essendon Place, Essendon, Hrt
Estcourt House, Shipton Moyne, Gls
Etal Manor, Ford, Nbl
Etherley Lodge, Etherley, Dur
Etherow House, Hollingworth, Chs
Ethy, St Winnow, Con
Ettington Park, Ettington, War
Eusemere, Pooley Bridge, Wes
Euston Hall, Euston, Sfk
Euxton Hall, Euxton, Lan
Evenley Hall, Evenley, Nth
Evercreech House, Evercreech, Som
Everdon Hall, Little Everdon, Nth
Everingham Park, Everingham, Yks
Everlands, Ide Hill, Ken
Everton Grange, Milford on Sea, Ham
Ewart Park, Doddington, Nbl
Ewell Manor, West Farleigh, Ken
Ewelme Park, Swyncombe, Oxf
Ewhurst Park, Ewhurst, Ham
Ewood Hall, Mytholmroyd, Yks
Exbourne Manor House, Exbourne, Dev
Exmoor, Exmoor, Som
Exton Park, Exton, Rut
Eyam Hall, Eyam, Dby
Eydon Hall, Eydon, Nth
Eyford Park, Eyford, Gls
Eynsham Hall, Eynsham, Oxf
Eyton Hall, Eyton, Hef
Eyton Hall, Eyton on the Weald Moors, Sal
Eywood, Titley, Hef

INDEX OF ENGLISH COUNTRY HOUSES

Faccombe Manor House, Faccombe, Ham
Faceby Manor, Faceby, Yks
Failand House, Wraxall, Som
Faintree Hall, Chetton, Sal
Fair Oak Lodge, Fair Oak, Ham
Fair Oak Park, Fair Oak, Ham
Fairchildes, Chelsham, Sry
Fairfield, Lymington, Ham
Fairfield, Peterchurch, Hef
Fairfield, Stogursey, Som
Fairford Park, Fairford, Gls
Fairhill, Shipbourne, Ken
Fairlawne, Plaxtol, Ken
Fairlight Hall, Fairlight, Ssx
Fairthorne Manor, Curdridge, Ham
Fallapit, East Allington, Dev
Falloden Hall, Embleton, Nbl
Fanshaws, Hertford, Hrt
Farfield Hall, Addingham, Yks
Faringdon House, Faringdon, Brk
Farington Lodge, Farington, Lan
Farleigh House, Farleigh Hungerford, Som
Farleigh House, Farleigh Wallop, Ham
Farley Court, Farley Hill, Brk
Farley Hall, Farley, Sts
Farley Hill Place, Farley Hill, Brk
Farley Moor, Binfield, Brk
Farm Hill House, Stroud, Gls
Farmhill Park, Stroud, Gls
Farnah Hall, Duffield, Dby
Farnborough Hall, Farnborough, War
Farnham Castle, Farnham, Sry
Farnham Park, Farnham Royal, Bkm
Farnhams Hall, Ware, Hrt
Farnley Hall, Farnley near Otley, Yks
Farringdon House, Farringdon, Dev
Farringford House, Freshwater, Ham
Fartherwell, Ryarsh, Ken
Farthinghoe Lodge, Farthinghoe, Nth
Faulkbourne Hall, Faulkbourne, Ess
Fawkham Manor, Fawkham, Ken
Fawley Court, Fawley, Bkm
Fawley Manor, Little Fawley, Brk
Fawsley, Fawsley, Nth
Featherstone Castle, Haltwhistle, Nbl
Felbrigg Hall, Felbrigg, Nfk
Feldemore, Abinger, Sry
Felix Hall, Kelvedon, Ess
Felley Priory, Felley, Ntt
Felmersham Grange, Felmersham, Bdf
Felthorpe Hall, Felthorpe, Nfk
Felton Park, Felton, Nbl
Feltwell Lodge, Feltwell, Nfk
Feniton Court, Feniton, Dev
Fenton, Doddington, Nbl
Fenton House, Hampstead, Mdx
Fergus Hill, Kirklinton, Cul
Fermyn Woods Hall, Brigstock, Nth
Fern Hill, Hawley, Ham
Fern Hill, Wootton, Ham

Ferne, Donhead St Andrew, Wil
Ferney Hall, Clungunford, Sal
Fernhill Hall, Whittington, Sal
Fernhill, Melton, Sfk
Fernhill Park, Cranbourne, Brk
Field, Compton, Sry
Field Dalling Hall, Field Dalling, Nfk
Field Place, Warnham, Ssx
Field Place, Whiteshill, Gls
Fifehead House, Fifehead Magdalen, Dor
Filby House, Filby, Nfk
Fillingham Castle, Fillingham, Lin
Fillongley Grange, Fillongley, War
Fillongley Hall, Fillongley, War
Fillongley Lodge, Fillongley, War
Fillongley Mount, Fillongley, War
Finborough Hall, Great Finborough, Sfk
Finchcox, Kilndown, Ken
Finedon Hall, Finedon, Nth
Fineshade Abbey, Fineshade, Nth
Finkley House, Knights Enham, Ham
Finningley Park, Austerfield, Yks
Finsthwaite House, Finsthwaite, Lan
Firby Hall, Bedale, Yks
Firby Hall, Westow, Yks
Firle Place, West Firle, Ssx
Firs (The), Hampstead, Mdx
Fishleigh, Hatherleigh, Dev
Fishwick Hall, Preston, Lan
Fitz Hall, Iping, Ssx
Fitz Manor, Fitz, Sal
Fitzharrys Manor, Abingdon, Brk
Fitzhead Court, Fitzhead, Som
Flasby Hall, Gargrave, Yks
Flass, Maulds Meaburn, Wes
Flaxley Abbey, Flaxley, Gls
Fledborough Hall, Holyport, Brk
Fleet House, Fleet, Dor
Fleets (The), Rylstone, Yks
Flete, Holbeton, Dev
Flimwell Grange, Kilndown, Ken
Flintham Hall, Flintham, Ntt
Flitwick Manor, Flitwick, Bdf
Flixton Hall, Flixton, Sfk
Flore House, Flore, Nth
Flosh (The), Cleator, Cul
Flower Lilies (The), Windley Township, Dby
Foley House, Maidstone, Ken
Foliejon Park, Winkfield, Brk
Folkington Manor, Folkington, Ssx
Fonthill Abbey, Fonthill Gifford, Wil
Fonthill House, Chilmark, Wil
Fontmell Parva, Child Okeford, Dor
Footherley Hall, Shenstone, Sts
Foots Cray Place, Foots Cray, Ken
Forcett Park, Forcett, Yks
Ford Castle, Ford, Nbl
Ford Hall, Chapel en le Frith, Dby
Ford Manor, Lingfield, Sry
Forde Abbey, Thorncombe, Dor

16

INDEX OF ENGLISH COUNTRY HOUSES

Fordham Abbey, Fordham, Cam
Forehill House, Alvechurch, Wor
Foremark Hall, Foremark, Dby
Forest Farm, Cranbourne, Brk
Forest Hall, High Ongar, Ess
Forest House, Nuthurst, Ssx
Forest Lodge, Binfield, Brk
Foresters Lodge, Wolsingham, Dur
Formby Hall, Formby, Lan
Forthampton Court, Forthampton, Gls
Forty Hall, Enfield, Mdx
Fosbury Manor, Fosbury, Wil
Foscombe, Ashleworth, Gls
Foscott Manor House, Foscott, Bkm
Foston Hall, Foston, Yks
Foston Hall, Scropton, Dby
Foulden Hall, Foulden, Nfk
Four Ashes Hall, Enville, Sts
Fowberry Tower, Chatton, Nbl
Fowey Hall, Fowey, Con
Fowley, Bramshott, Ham
Fownhope Court, Fownhope, Hef
Fox Hill, Earley, Brk
Foxcote House, Ilmington, War
Foxhunt Manor, Waldron, Ssx
Foxley-Henning, Raughton Head, Cul
Foxley, Yazor, Hef
Foxwarren Park, Wisley, Sry
Foys, Chetnole, Dor
Fradswell Hall, Fradswell, Sts
Framfield Place, Framfield, Ssx
Framingham Hall, Framingham Pigot, Nfk
Framingham Manor House, Framingham Pigot, Nfk
Frampton Court, Frampton, Dor
Frampton Court, Frampton on Severn, Gls
Frampton Grange, Frampton Cotterell, Gls
Frampton Grange, Frampton on Severn, Gls
Frampton Hall, Frampton, Lin
Franks, Horton Kirby, Ken
Frankton Grange, Cockshutt, Sal
Frant Court, Frant, Ssx
Fredville, Nonington, Ken
Freeford Hall, Lichfield, Sts
Freeland House, Freeland, Oxf
Frensham Hall, Frensham, Sry
Frensham Place, Frensham, Sry
Frensham, Rolvenden, Ken
Freshford Manor, Freshford, Som
Friar Park, Henley on Thames, Oxf
Friarage (The), Yarm, Yks
Friars (The), Aylesford, Ken
Frickley Hall, Clayton with Frickley, Yks
Frimley Park, Frimley, Sry
Frimstone, Bramshott, Ham
Fring Hall, Fring, Nfk
Fringford Manor House, Fringford, Oxf
Friningham Lodge, Thurnham, Ken
Friston Place, Friston, Ssx
Frittenden House, Frittenden, Ken
Fritwell Manor House, Fritwell, Oxf

Frocester Manor House, Frocester, Gls
Frogmore Hall, Aston, Hrt
Frogmore Park, Yateley, Ham
Frognal House, Hampstead, Mdx
Frome Whitfield House, Stinsford, Dor
Froyle House, Froyle, Ham
Froyle Place, Froyle, Ham
Fulbeck Hall, Fulbeck, Lin
Fulbourn Manor, Fulbourn, Cam
Fulford Hall, Fulford, Yks
Fulham Palace, Fulham, Mdx
Fulmer Hall, Fulmer, Bkm
Fulmer Place, Fulmer, Bkm
Funtington House, Funtington, Ssx
Furneux Pelham Hall, Furneux Pelham, Hrt
Fursdon, Cadbury, Dev
Fursdon, Egg Buckland, Dev
Furze Hill, North Walsham, Nfk
Furzebrook House, Church Knowle, Dor

Gaddesby Hall, Gaddesby, Lei
Gaddesden Place, Great Gaddesden, Hrt
Gaddon House, Uffculme, Dev
Gage (The), Little Berkhamsted, Hrt
Gaines, Whitbourne, Hef
Galesyke, Nether Wasdale, Cul
Gallowhill Hall, Bolam, Nbl
Gangmoor, Hampstead, Mdx
Ganton Hall, Ganton, Yks
Garboldisham Hall, Garboldisham, Nfk
Garboldisham Manor, Garboldisham, Nfk
Garendon Park, Garendon, Lei
Gargrave House, Gargrave, Yks
Garlenick, Creed, Con
Garlog's, Nether Wallop, Ham
Garnons, Mansell Gamage, Hef
Garnstone Castle, Weobley, Hef
Garrowby Hall, Kirby Underdale, Yks
Garswood Hall, Ashton in Makerfield, Lan
Garth Marr, Castle Carrock, Cul
Gatacre Hall, Claverley, Sal
Gatacre Park, Tuck Hill, Sal
Gatcombe House, Gatcombe, Ham
Gatcombe, Minchinhampton, Gls
Gate Burton Hall, Gate Burton, Lin
Gate, Dent, Yks
Gate House, Eskdale, Cul
Gateford Hill, Gateford, Ntt
Gatherley Castle, Middleton Tyas, Yks
Gatley Park, Leinthall Earles, Hef
Gatton Manor, Abinger, Sry
Gaunt's House, Hinton Martell, Dor
Gaveston Place, Nuthurst, Ssx
Gawdy Hall, Harleston, Nfk
Gawthorpe Hall, Padiham, Lan
Gayhurst, Gayhurst, Bkm
Gaynes Hall, Great Staughton, Hun
Gaynes Park, Theydon Garnon, Ess
Gayton Hall, Gayton, Nfk
Gayton Hall, Upton Bishop, Hef

Gaywood Hall, Gaywood, Nfk
Gedding Hall, Gedding, Sfk
Gedling House, Gedling, Ntt
Geldeston Hall, Geldeston, Nfk
Gennings, Hunton, Ken
Gestingthorpe Hall, Gestingthorpe, Ess
Gibside Hall, Wolsingham, Dur
Gidleigh Park, Gidleigh, Dev
Gifford Hall, Broughton Gifford, Wil
Gifford's Hall, Wickhambrook, Sfk
Giffords Hall, Stoke by Nayland, Sfk
Gilgarran, Distington, Cul
Gillingham Hall, Gillingham, Nfk
Gilmonby Hall, Bowes, Yks
Gilston Park, Gilston, Hrt
Girsby Manor, Burgh upon Bain, Lin
Gisborough Hall, Guisborough, Yks
Gisburne Park, Gisburne, Yks
Glassenbury, Cranbrook, Ken
Glaston House, Glaston, Lei
Glaston House, Glaston, Rut
Glazeley Hall, Glazeley, Sal
Gledstone, West Marton, Yks
Glemham Hall, Little Glemham, Sfk
Glen Aln, Edlingham, Nbl
Glen Court, Llanllowell, Mon
Glen Parva Grange, Glen Parva, Lei
Glen (The), Scalby, Yks
Glen View House, Downside, Som
Glencot, Wookey Hole, Som
Glendon Hall, Glendon, Nth
Glenmonnow House, Garway, Hef
Glenthorne, Countisbury, Dev
Glenusk, Llanhennock, Mon
Glevering Park, Hacheston, Sfk
Gloucester Palace, Gloucester, Gls
Glympton Park, Glympton, Oxf
Glynde Place, Glynde, Ssx
Glyndebourne, Glynde, Ssx
Glynley House, Westham, Ssx
Glynn House, Cardinham, Con
Gnaton Hall, Newton Ferrers, Dev
Godinton, Great Chart, Ken
Godmersham Park, Godmersham, Ken
Gog-Magog Hills House, Stapleford, Cam
Goldicote, Alderminster, War
Goldingham Hall, Bulmer, Ess
Goldington Bury, Goldington, Bdf
Goldington Hall, Goldington, Bdf
Goldingtons, Sarratt, Hrt
Gonalston Hall, Gonalston, Ntt
Goodnestone Park, Goodnestone, Ken
Goodrich Court, Goodrich, Hef
Goodwood, Boxgrove, Ssx
Gopsall Park, Gopsall, Lei
Gore Court, Otham, Ken
Gorhambury, St Albans, Hrt
Gosberton House, Gosberton, Lin
Gosfield Hall, Gosfield, Ess
Gothelney Manor, Charlinch, Som

Gotton House, West Monkton, Som
Goudhurst Grange, Goudhurst, Ken
Government House, St Saviour, Jersey
Goytrey Hall, Goytrey, Mon
Grace Dieu Manor, Belton, Lei
Grafham Grange, Bramley, Sry
Grafton Hall, Grafton, Chs
Grafton Manor, Grafton Regis, Nth
Graig (The), Llantilio-Crossenny, Mon
Grainsby Hall, Grainsby, Lin
Grainvlle Manor, St Saviour, Jersey
Grange (The), Bow, Dev
Grange (The), Casterton, Wes
Grange (The), Chetnole, Dor
Grange (The), Collingtree, Nth
Grange (The), Hockliffe, Bdf
Grange (The), Kingham, Oxf
Grange (The), Marnhull, Dor
Grange (The), Northington, Ham
Grange (The), Rockbeare, Dev
Grange (The), Thurston, Sfk
Grange (The), Woodhouse Eaves, Lei
Grangewood Hall, Nether Seal, Dby
Gransden Hall, Great Gransden, Hun
Grantlands, Uffculme, Dev
Grantley Hall, Winksley, Yks
Grassyard Hall, Caton, Lan
Grateley House, Grateley, Ham
Graythwaite Hall, Satterthwaite, Lan
Great Ambrook, Ipplepen, Dev
Great Barford House, Great Barford, Bdf
Great Bounds, Bidborough, Ken
Great Bromley Lodge, Great Bromley, Ess
Great Claydons, East Hanningfield, Ess
Great Codham Hall, Wethersfield, Ess
Great Dixter, Northiam, Ssx
Great Frenches Park, Crawley Down, Ssx
Great Fulford, Dunsford, Dev
Great Glemham House, Great Glemham, Sfk
Great Houghton Hall, Great Houghton, Nth
Great Madeley Manor House, Great Madeley, Sts
Great Maytham, Rolvenden, Ken
Great Milton Manor House, Great Milton, Oxf
Great Oaks, Goring Heath, Oxf
Great Ote Hall, Wivelsfield, Ssx
Great Testwood, Eling, Ham
Great Thurlow Hall, Great Thurlow, Sfk
Great Wood, Mylor, Con
Great Wratting Hall, Great Wratting, Sfk
Greatford Hall, Greatford, Lin
Greaves Hall, Bank, Lan
Grebby Hall, Scremby, Lin
Green Hammerton Hall, Whixley, Yks
Green (The), Bacton, Hef
Green's Norton Hall, Green's Norton, Nth
Greendale, Clyst St Mary, Dev
Greenham Hall, Stawley, Som
Greenham Lodge, Greenham, Brk
Greenlands, Hambleden, Bkm
Greenstead Hall, Halstead, Ess

INDEX OF ENGLISH COUNTRY HOUSES

Greensted Hall, Greensted juxta Ongar, Ess
Greenthorne, Edgworth, Lan
Greenway Bank, Norton in the Moors, Sts
Greenway House, Churston Ferrers, Dev
Greenway (The), Shurdington, Gls
Greenwell Ford, Lanchester, Dur
Greenwich Palace, Greenwich, Ken
Greenwood, Durley, Ham
Grendon Hall, Grendon Underwood, Bkm
Grendon Hall, Grendon, War
Grenehurst Park, Capel, Sry
Grenofen, |Whitchurch, Dev
Greppenhall Hall, Grappenhall, Chs
Gresham Hall, Gresham, Nfk
Gressenhall House, Gressenhall, Nfk
Grey Friars, Dunwich, Sfk
Grey Friars, Winchelsea, Ssx
Greyfriars, Storrington, Ssx
Greys Court, Rotherfield Greys, Oxf
Greystoke Castle, Greystoke, Cul
Greywell Hill House, Greywell, Ham
Grimeshill, Middleton, Wes
Grimshaw Hall, Knowle, War
Grimsthorpe Castle, Edenham, Lin
Grimston Court, Dunnington, Yks
Grimston Hall, Garton with Grimston, Yks
Grimston Park, Kirkby Wharfe, Yks
Grimstone Manor, Gilling, Yks
Grinkle Park, Easington, Yks
Grinshill Grange, Grinshill, Sal
Grinton Lodge, Grinton, Yks
Grittleton House, Grittleton, Wil
Grizedale Hall, Satterthwaite, Lan
Groombridge Place, Old Groombridge, Ken
Groton House, Groton, Sfk
Grove Hall, Grove, Ntt
Grove Park, Bubrooke, War
Grove Park, Yoxford, Sfk
Grove Place, Nursling, Ham
Grove (The), Chalfont St Giles, Bkm
Grove (The), Great Glemham, Sfk
Grove (The), Little Bealings, Sfk
Grove (The), The Slad, Gls
Grove (The), Walsham-le-Willows, Sfk
Grovehurst, Pembury, Ken
Groveley House, Cofton Hackett, Wor
Grundisburgh Hall, Grundisburgh, Sfk
Guilsborough Court, Guilsborough, Nth
Guilsborough Grange, Guilsborough, Nth
Guilsborough Hall, Guilsborough, Nth
Guiting Grange, Guiting Power, Gls
Gumley Hall, Gumley, Lei
Gunby Hall, Gunby St Peter, Lin
Gunthorpe Hall, Gunthorpe, Nfk
Gunton Old Hall, Gunton, Sfk
Gunton Park, Gunton, Nfk
Guy's Cliffe, Warwick, War
Guyzance Hall, Acklington, Nbl

Haccombe, House, Haccombe, Dev
Hackenthorpe Hall, Hackenthorpe, Dby
Hackford Hall, Hackford, Nfk
Hackness Grange, Hackness, Yks
Hackness Hall, Hackness, Yks
Hackthorn Hall, Hackthorn, Lin
Hackwood Park, Basingstoke, Ham
Haconby Hall, Haconby, Lin
Haddiscoe Hall, Haddiscoe, Nfk
Haddon Hall, Nether Haddon, Dby
Haddon Lodge, Caundle Stourton, Dor
Hadham Hall, Little Hadham, Hrt
Hadleigh Hall, Hadleigh, Sfk
Hadlow Castle, Hadlow, Ken
Hadlow Park, Hadlow, Ken
Hadspen House, Pitcombe, Som
Hagley Court, Lugwardine, Hef
Hagley Hall, Hagley, Wor
Haie (The), Newnham, Gls
Haigh Hall, Haigh, Lan
Haighton House, Haighton, Lan
Haile Hall, Haile, Cul
Haines Hill, Hurst, Brk
Hainton Hall, Hainton, Lin
Hale Hall, Hale, Lan
Hale Park, Hale, Ham
Halecote, Witherslack, Wes
Hales Hall, Cheadle, Sts
Hales Hall, Hales, Sts
Halford Manor House, Halford, War
Hall Barn, Beaconsfield, Bkm
Hall, Bishops Tawton, Dev
Hall Place, Bexley, Ken
Hall Place, Hascombe, Sry
Hall Place, Hurley, Brk
Hall Place, Leigh, Ken
Hall Place, Sparsholt, Brk
Hall (The), Binfield, Brk
Hall (The), Bradford on Avon, Wil
Hall (The), Marston on Dove, Dby
Hall (The), Winscombe, Som
Hallaton Manor, Hallaton, Lei
Hallfield, Wetherby, Yks
Hallington Demesne, St Oswald in Lee, Nbl
Hallow Park, Hallow, Wor
Hallsannery, Bideford, Dev
Halnaby Hall, Croft, Yks
Halsnead Hall, Whiston, Lan
Halston Hall, Whittington, Sal
Halsway Manor, Bicknoller, Som
Halswell Park, Goathurst, Som
Halton Hall, Aughton, Lan
Halton Park, Aughton, Lan
Ham House, Petersham, Sry
Ham Manor, Angmering, Ssx
Ham, Weston Peverel, Dev
Hamble Cliff, Netley Abbey, Ham
Hambleton Hall, Hambleton, Rut
Hambrook House, Funtington, Ssx
Hames Hall, Papcastle, Cul

Hammerwood Park, Hammerwood, Ssx
Hammonds, Checkendon, Oxf
Hampden House, Great Hampden, Bkm
Hampsfield, Lindale, Lan
Hampton Court, Hope under Dinmore, Hef
Hampton Hall, Hampton, Chs
Hampton Hall, Worthen, Sal
Hampton Manor, Hampton in Arden, War
Hampton, Seale, Sry
Hamptons, West Peckham, Ken
Hamsell Manor, Eridge Green, Ssx
Hamstead Marshall Park, Hamstead Marshall, Brk
Hamsterley Hall, Medomsley, Dur
Hamswell House, Cold Ashton, Gls
Hanbury Hall, Hanbury, Wor
Handcross Park, Slaugham, Ssx
Hanford House, Hanford, Dor
Hannington Hall, Hannington, Wil
Hanslope Park, Hanslope, Bkm
Hanwell Castle, Hanwell, Oxf
Hanworth Hall, Hanworth, Nfk
Hapstead, Buckfastleigh, Dev
Harbottle Castle, Holystone, Nbl
Harbury House, Harbury, War
Harcombe, Chudleigh, Dev
Harcourt, Stanton, Sal
Harden Grange, Bingley, Yks
Hardenhuish Park, Hardenhuish, Wil
Hardingham Hall, Hardingham, Nfk
Hardres Court, Upper Hardres, Ken
Hardwick Court, Chepstow, Mon
Hardwick Hall, Ault Hucknall, Dby
Hardwick Hall, Ellesmere, Sal
Hardwick Hall, Sedgefield, Dur
Hardwick House, Hardwick, Sfk
Hardwick House, Whitchurch, Oxf
Hardwicke Court, Hardwicke, Gls
Hare Hill, Over Alderley, Chs
Hare Park, Swaffham Bulbeck, Cam
Hareby Manor, Hareby, Lin
Hareden, Slaidburn, Yks
Harefield Grove, Harefield, Mdx
Harefield Place, Harefield, Mdx
Harehope Hall, Eglingham, Nbl
Haremere Hall, Etchingham, Ssx
Harescombe Grange, Harescombe, Gls
Haresfield Court, Haresfield, Gls
Haresfoot, Great Berkhamsted, Hrt
Harewood House, Harewood, Yks
Harewood Park, Harewood, Hef
Hargate Hall, Wormhill, Dby
Hargham Hall, Hargham, Nfk
Harlaxton Manor, Harlaxton, Lin
Harlestone House, Harlestone, Nth
Harleyford House, Marlow, Bkm
Harlsey Hall, East Harlsey, Yks
Harlyn House, St Merryn, Con
Harnhill Manor House, Harnhill, Gls
Harperley Park, North Bedburn, Dur
Harpford House, Harpford, Dev

Harpole Hall, Harpole, Nth
Harpsden Court, Harpsden, Oxf
Harptree Court, East Harptree, Som
Harrington Hall, Harrington, Lin
Harrold Hall, Harrold, Bdf
Harrowden Hall, Great Harrowden, Nth
Harsfold Manor, Wisborough Green, Ssx
Harston Manor House, Harston, Cam
Hartford House, Bedlington, Nbl
Hartforth Hall, Gilling West near Richmond, Yks
Hartham Park, Corsham, Wil
Hartland Abbey, Hartland, Dev
Hartlebury Castle, Hartlebury, Wor
Hartpury House, Hartpury, Gls
Hartsholme Hall, Skellingthorpe, Lin
Hartwell House, Hartwell, Bkm
Haselbech Hall, Hazelbeech, Nth
Haseley Court, Little Haseley, Oxf
Haseley Manor House, Haseley, War
Hasells Hall, Sandy, Bdf
Haselour Hall, Harlaston, Sts
Hasfield Court, Hasfield, Gls
Hasketon Manor, Hasketon, Sfk
Haslington Hall, Haslington, Chs
Hassobury, Farnham, Ess
Hassop Hall, Hassop, Dby
Hatch Park, Hatch Beauchamp, Som
Hatchford Park, Cobham, Sry
Hatchlands, East Clandon, Sry
Hatfield Court, Hatfield, Hef
Hatfield House, Hatfield, Hrt
Hatherley Court, Down Hatherley, Gls
Hatherop Castle, Hatherop, Gls
Hatherton Hall, Gailey, Sts
Hatherton House, Hatherton, Chs
Hatley Park, Hatley St George, Cam
Hatt, Botus Fleming, Con
Hatton House, Hatton, War
Hatton, Shifnal, Sal
Haughley Park, Haughley, Sfk
Haughton Castle, Humshaugh, Nbl
Haughton Hall, Haughton, Chs
Haughton Hall, Shifnal, Sal
Hauxwell Hall, Hauxwell, Yks
Haverland Hall, Haveringland, Nfk
Hawkhills, Easingwold, Yks
Hawkshead, Bolton le Sands, Lan
Hawksworth Hall, Esholt, Yks
Hawkwell Place, Pembury, Ken
Hawley House, Hawley, Ham
Hawthorne House, Hampstead, Mdx
Hayne House, Tiverton, Dev
Hayne, Stowford, Dev
Haynford Hall, Hainford, Nfk
Hays, Sedgehill, Wil
Hayton House, Hayton, Cul
Hazel Manor, Ubley, Som
Hazelby, East Woodhay, Ham
Hazelgrove, Queen Camel, Som
Hazlewood Castle, Tadcaster, Yks

Heacham Hall, Heacham, Nfk
Headington Hill House, Oxford, Oxf
Headington House, Headington, Oxf
Headlam Hall, Darlington, Dur
Headley Court, Headley, Sry
Headley Grove, Headley, Sry
Headley Park, Headley, Ham
Headley Park, Headley, Sry
Heads Nook, Faugh, Cul
Healaugh Manor, Healaugh, Yks
Heale House, Curry Rivel, Som
Heale House, Upper Woodford, Wil
Healey Hall, Healey St John, Nbl
Heanton Satchville, Huish and Petrockstow, Dev
Heath End House, Hampstead, Mdx
Heath House, Leintwardine, Hef
Heath House (The), Upper Tean, Sts
Heath Old Hall, Warmfield cum Heath, Yks
Heath Place, Hartfield, Ssx
Heatherden, Waldron, Ssx
Heathfield Park, Heathfield, Ssx
Heathfield, Wolverley, Wor
Heathlands, Wokingham, Brk
Heaves, Levens, Wes
Heawood Hall, Nether Alderley, Chs
Heckfield Place, Heckfield, Ham
Heckington Hall, Heckington, Lin
Heckley House, Alnwick, Nbl
Hedenham Hall, Hedenham, Nfk
Hedgefield House, Ryton, Dur
Hedgerley Park, Hedgerley, Bkm
Hedingham Castle, Castle Hedingham, Ess
Hedsor House, Hedsor, Bkm
Heggatt Hall, Horstead, Nfk
Heightside House, Rawtenstall, Lan
Helbeck Hall, Hillbeck, Wes
Helidon House, Hellidon, Nth
Heligan, St Ewe, Con
Hellens, Much Marcle, Hef
Hellesdon House, Hellesdon, Nfk
Hellifield Peel, Long Preston, Yks
Helme Lodge, Natland, Wes
Helmingham Hall, Helmingham, Sfk
Helperby Hall, Brafferton, Yks
Hembury Fort House, Buckerell, Dev
Hemerdon House, Sparkwell, Dev
Hemingford Park, Hemingford Abbots, Hun
Hemingstone Hall, Hemingstone, Sfk
Hemploe (The), Welford, Nth
Hempstead Court, Hempstead, Gls
Hemsby Hall, Hemsby, Nfk
Henbury, Elham, Ken
Henbury House, Sturminster Marshall, Dor
Henbury Manor, Sturminster Marshall, Dor
Henbury Park, Henbury cum Pexall, Chs
Hendford Manor, Yeovil, Som
Hendre (The), Llangattock-Vibon-Abel, Mon
Hendred House, East Hendred, Brk
Hengar, St Tudy, Con
Hengherst, Woodchurch, Ken

Hengrave Hall, Hengrave, Sfk
Henham Hall, Henham, Sfk
Henlade House, Ruishton, Som
Henley Hall, Bitterley, Sal
Henley Park, Ash, Sry
Henlle Hall, Hengoed cum Gobowen, Sal
Henlow Grange, Henlow, Bdf
Henniker House, Fulham, Mdx
Hennor, Leominster, Hef
Hensleigh House, Tiverton, Dev
Henstead Hall, Henstead, Sfk
Hepple Whitefield, Rothbury, Nbl
Hereford Palace, Hereford, Hef
Hermeston Hall, Hodsock, Ntt
Hermitage (The), Burghill, Hef
Hermitage (The), Chester le Street, Dur
Hermitage (The), Thornton Watlass, Yks
Hermitage (The), West Malling, Ken
Heron Court, Hurn, Ham
Heron's Ghyll, High Hurstwood, Ssx
Herontye, East Grinstead, Ssx
Herriard Park, Herriard, Ham
Herringby Hall, Stokesby, Nfk
Herringfleet Hall, Herringfleet, Sfk
Herrington, Winterbourne Herrington, Dor
Herringswell Manor House, Herringswell, Sfk
Herringswell Place, Herringswell, Sfk
Herstmonceaux Castle, Herstmonceaux, Ssx
Herstmonceaux Place, Herstmonceaux, Ssx
Hesket Hall, Hesket New Market, Cul
Hesley Hall, Harworth, Ntt
Hesleyside, Bellingham, Nbl
Heslington Hall, Heslington, Yks
Hestercombe, Kingston near Taunton, Som
Hethel Hall, Hethel, Nfk
Hethersett Hall, Hethersett, Nfk
Hethersett Old Hall, Hethersett, Nfk
Hethfelton, East Stoke, Dor
Heveningham Hall, Heveningham, Sfk
Hever Castle, Hever, Ken
Hewell Grange, Tardebigge, Wor
Hewshott House, Bramshott, Ham
Hexgreave Park, Farnsfield, Ntt
Hexton Manor, Hexton, Hrt
Heybridge, Checkley, Sts
Heydon Hall, Heydon, Nfk
Heyes (The), Grappenhall, Chs
Heyes (The), Warrington, Lan
Heyford Hills, Nether Heyford, Nth
Heyford Manor House, Nether Heyford, Nth
Heysham Hall, Heysham, Lan
Heysham House, Heysham, Lan
Heysham Lodge, Heysham, Lan
Heytesbury House, Heytesbury, Wil
Hickleton Hall, Hickleton, Yks
High Ashes, Abinger, Sry
High Beeches, Slaugham, Ssx
High Borrans, Windermere, Wes
High Bullen, Chittlehamholt, Dev
High Canons, Shenley, Hrt

High Close, Rydal and Loughrigg, Wes
High Coxlease, Lyndhurst, Ham
High Cross, Framfield, Ssx
High Down, Pirton, Hrt
High Elms, Downe, Ken
High Green, Bellingham, Nbl
High Grove, Eastcote, Mdx
High Hall, Nettlestead, Sfk
High Hall, Pamphill, Dor
High Head Castle, Ivegill, Cul
High House, Hawkshead, Lan
High Legh Hall, High Legh, Chs
High Warden, Warden, Nbl
Higham Bury, Higham Gobion, Bdf
Higham House, Salehurst, Ssx
Higham, Setmurthy, Cul
Highclere Castle, Highclere, Ham
Highcliff Castle, Highcliff, Ham
Highfield Hall, Leek Frith, Sts
Highfield, Husbands Bosworth, Lei
Highfield Park, Heckfield, Ham
Highfield, Shoreham, Ken
Highfields, Buerton, Chs
Highfure, Billingshurst, Ssx
Highgrove, Tetbury Upton, Gls
Highland Court, Patrixbourne, Ken
Highlands, Grazeley, Brk
Highley Manor, Balcombe, Ssx
Highmoor Hall, Highmore Cross, Oxf
Highnam Court, Highnam, Gls
Hilborough Hall, Hilborough, Nfk
Hilcote Hall, Chebsey, Sts
Hildersham Hall, Hildersham, Cam
Hilderstone Hall, Hilderstone, Sts
Hildon House, East Tytherley, Ham
Hill Court, Hill, Gls
Hill Court, Walford, Hef
Hill End House, Mottram in Longdendale, Chs
Hill Hall, Theydon Mount, Ess
Hill House, Otterhampton, Som
Hill House, Winterton, Nfk
Hill House, Yetminster, Dor
Hill, Slinfold, Ssx
Hill (The), Abergavenny, Mon
Hill Top, New Hutton, Wes
Hillam Hall, Hillam, Yks
Hillersdon House, Cullompton, Dev
Hillfield Hall, Solihull, War
Hillfields, Burghfield, Brk
Hillington Hall, Hillington, Nfk
Hilston Park, St Maughans, Mon
Hilton Park, Hilton, Sts
Himbleton Manor, Himbleton, Wor
Himley Hall, Himley, Sts
Hinchelsea, Brockenhurst, Ham
Hinchingbrooke, Huntingdon, Hun
Hindlip Hall, Hindlip, Wor
Hindringham Hall, Hindringham, Nfk
Hinstock Hall, Hinstock, Sal
Hintlesham Hall, Hintlesham, Sfk

Hinton Abbey, Hinton Charterhouse, Som
Hinton Admiral, Hinton, Ham
Hinton Ampner House, Hinton Ampner, Ham
Hinton Daubnay, Catherington, Ham
Hinton Hall, Pontesbury, Sal
Hinton House, Hinton Charterhouse, Som
Hinton House, Hinton St George, Som
Hinton House, Woodford cum Membris, Nth
Hinton Manor, Catherington, Ham
Hinton Manor, Hinton Waldrist, Brk
Hinton St Mary Manor House, Hinton St Mary, Dor
Hints Hall, Hints, Sts
Hinwick Hall, Podington, Bdf
Hinwick House, Podington, Bdf
Hinxton Hall, Hinxton, Cam
Hirst Priory, Belton by Doncaster, Lin
Histon Manor, Histon, Cam
Hitcham House, Hitcham, Bkm
Hitchin Priory, Hitchin, Hrt
Hoar Cross Hall, Hoar Cross, Sts
Hoath (The), Chiddingstone, Ken
Hob Ground Hall, Kirby Misperton, Yks
Hobland Hall, Bradwell, Sfk
Hockham Hall, Hockham, Nfk
Hockley Sole, Capel le Ferne, Ken
Hoddington House, Upton Grey, Ham
Hodnet Hall, Hodnet, Sal
Hodsock Priory, Hodsock, Ntt
Hoghton Tower, Hoghton, Lan
Holbeck Ghyll, Troutbeck, Wes
Holbeck Manor, Ashby Puerorum, Lin
Holbrook Grange, Little Lawford, War
Holbrook Hall, Holbrook, Dby
Holbrook House, Bratton Seymour, Som
Holbrook Park, Horsham, Ssx
Holcombe Court, Holcombe Rogus, Dev
Holdcroft, Blunsdon St Andrew, Wil
Holden Clough, Bolton by Bowland, Yks
Holdenby House, Holdenby, Nth
Hole Park, Rolvenden, Ken
Holehird, Windermere, Wes
Holesfoot Lodge, Maulds Meaburn, Wes
Holeyn Hall, Wylam, Nbl
Holfield Grange, Coggeshall, Ess
Holker Hall, Lower Holker, Lan
Hollam, Dulverton, Som
Hollin Hall, Littlethorpe, Yks
Hollingbourne House, Hollingbourne, Ken
Hollington House, Woolton Hill, Ham
Hollonds (The), Langton Green, Ken
Holloway (The), Redditch, Wor
Holly Bush Hall, Newborough, Sts
Holly Hill, Hartfield, Ssx
Holly Hurst, Riddings, Dby
Holly Lodge, Burgh Apton, Nfk
Holly Lodge, Moulton, Nth
Holly Spring, Bracknell, Brk
Hollyberry Hall, Allesley, War
Hollywood Tower, Henbury, Gls
Holm Hill, Hawksdale, Cul

Holmbush, Colgate, Ssx
Holme Hale Hall, Holme Hale, Nfk
Holme House, Holme next the Sea, Nfk
Holme Pierrepont Hall, Holme Pierrepont, Ntt
Holme Priory, East Holme, Dor
Holmer Park, Holmer, Hef
Holmesland, Botley, Ham
Holmewood, Langton Green, Ken
Holmrook Hall, Holmrook, Cul
Holmsted Manor, Staplefield, Ssx
Holmwood Place, Four Elms, Ken
Holnest Park, Holnest, Dor
Holnicote, Selworthy, Som
Holt Castle, Holt, Wor
Holt Hall, Holt, Nfk
Holt Lodge, Holt, Nfk
Holt Manor House, Holt, Wil
Holtby Hall, Hornby, Yks
Holton Hall, Holton le Moor, Lin
Holton Hall, Holton, Sfk
Holton Park, Holton, Oxf
Holwell Bury, Shillington, Bdf
Holwell Manor House, Holwell, Dor
Holwell, Whitchurch, Dev
Holwood, Keston, Ken
Holy Wath, Coniston, Lan
Holy Wells, Ipswich, Sfk
Holywell Hall, Careby Annby and Holywell, Lin
Holywell House, Swanmore, Ham
Homend, Stretton Grandison, Hef
Homington House, Homington, Wil
Homme House, Much Marcle, Hef
Honiley Hall, Honiley, War
Honing Hall, Honing, Nfk
Honingham Hall, Honingham, Nfk
Honington Hall, Honington, Lin
Honington Park, Honington, War
Hoo (The), Kimpton, Hrt
Hooke Court, Hooke, Dor
Hooke (The), Chailey, Ssx
Hoole Hall, Hoole, Chs
Hooton Pagnell Hall, Hooton Pagnell, Yks
Hopleys (The), Horningsheath, Sfk
Hoppyland Park, South Bedburn, Dur
Hopton Court, Hopton Wafers, Sal
Hopton Court, Leigh, Wor
Hopton Hall, Hopton, Dby
Hopwood Hall, Heywood, Lan
Horham Hall, Thaxted, Ess
Horkesley Park, Great Horkesley, Ess
Hornby Castle, Hornby, Lan
Hornby Castle, Hornby, Yks
Horringer Court, Horningsheath, Sfk
Horringer Manor, Horningsheath, Sfk
Horseleas, Bradfield, Brk
Horsenden Manor House, Horsenden, Bkm
Horsey Hall, Horsey, Nfk
Horsford Manor, Horsford, Nfk
Horsington House, Horsington, Som
Horsington Manor, Horsington, Som

Horsley Hall, Bishop Auckland, Dur
Horsley Hall, Eccleshall, Sts
Horstead Hall, Horstead, Nfk
Horsted Place, Little Horsted, Ssx
Horswell, South Milton, Dev
Horton Hall, Horton, Gls
Horton Hall, Horton, Sts
Horton House, Horton, Nth
Horton Manor, Horton, Gls
Horwood House, Little Horwood, Bkm
Hotham Hall, North Cave, Yks
Hothfield Place, Hothfield, Ken
Hothorpe Hall, Hothorpe, Nth
Houghton Grange, Houghton, Hun
Houghton Hall, Houghton, Cul
Houghton Hall, Houghton, Nfk
Houghton Hall, Houghton Regis, Bdf
Houghton Hall, Sancton, Yks
Houghton Manor, Houghton, Hun
Hoveton Hall, Hoveton St Peter, Nfk
Hoveton House, Hoveton St John, Nfk
Hovingham Hall, Hovingham, Yks
How Caple Court, How Caple, Hef
Howbery Park, Crowmarsh Gifford, Oxf
Howbury Hall, Renhold, Bdf
Howden Dene, Corbridge, Nbl
Howden, Tiverton, Dev
Howe (The), Halstead, Ess
Howe (The), Windermere, Wes
Howick Hall, Howick, Nbl
Howletts, Ickham, Ken
Howsham Hall, Scrayingham, Yks
Huddington Court, Huddington, Wor
Hughenden Manor, Hughenden, Bkm
Hull Place, Sholden, Ken
Hulland Hall, Hulland, Dby
Hulton Park, Hulton, Lan
Hungerford Park, Hungerford, Brk
Hungerton Hall, Hungerton, Lin
Hunsdon Bury, Hunsdon, Hrt
Hunsdon House, Hunsdon, Hrt
Hunstanton Hall, Hunstanton, Nfk
Hunters Lodge, Hampstead, Mdx
Huntley Manor, Huntley, Gls
Hunton Court, Hunton, Ken
Huntroyde, Padiham, Lan
Huntsham Court, Huntsham, Dev
Hurdcott House, Baverstock, Wil
Hurlingham House, Fulham, Mdx
Hursley Park, Hursley, Ham
Hurst Lodge, Hurst, Brk
Hurstbourne Park, Hurstbourne Priors, Ham
Hurts Hall, Saxmundham, Sfk
Hurworth Grange, Darlington, Dur
Hurworth Moor, Hurworth on Tees, Dur
Hutton Bonville Hall, Hutton Bonville, Yks
Hutton Court, Hutton, Som
Hutton Hall, Guisborough, Yks
Hutton Hall, Long Marston, Yks
Hutton Hall, Penwortham, Lan

Hutton in the Forest, Hutton in the Forest, Cul
Hutton John, Greystoke, Cul
Huttons Ambo Hall, Huttons Ambo, Yks
Hyde Hall, Sawbridgeworth, Hrt
Hyde (The), Hyde, Bdf
Hyde (The), Ingatestone, Ess
Hyde (The), Slaugham, Ssx
Hylands, Widford, Ess
Hyning Hall, Warton, Lan

Ibbotsholme, Troutbeck, Wes
Ibstone House, Ibstone, Bkm
Ickleford Manor, Ickleford, Hrt
Ickworth Park, Ickworth, Sfk
Icomb Place, Icomb, Gls
Iden Manor, Staplehurst, Ken
Idlerocks, Moddershall, Sts
Idlicote House, Idlicote, War
Idsworth House, Idsworth, Ham
Ifield Hall, Ifield, Ssx
Iford Manor, Westwood, Wil
Ightham Court, Ightham, Ken
Ightham Mote, Ightham, Ken
Ightham Warren, Ightham, Ken
Ilmington Manor House, Ilmington, War
Ilsington House, Puddletown, Dor
Imberhorne Manor, East Grinstead, Ssx
Impington Hall, Impington, Cam
Ince Blundell Hall, Sefton, Lan
Ince Castle, St Stephens by Saltash, Con
Ince Hall, Ince, Chs
Indio House, Bovey Tracey, Dev
Ingatestone Hall, Ingatestone, Ess
Ingestre, Ingestre, Sts
Ingleborough Hall, Clapham, Yks
Ingleby Manor, Ingleby Greenhow, Yks
Inglethorpe Manor, Emneth, Nfk
Inglewood, Great Salkeld, Cul
Ingmanthorpe Hall, Kirk Deighton, Yks
Ingoldisthorpe Hall, Ingoldisthorpe, Nfk
Ingoldisthorpe Manor House, Ingoldisthorpe, Nfk
Ingon Grange, Snitterfield, War
Inholmes, Woodlands St Mary, Brk
Intwood Hall, Intwood, Nfk
Inwood, Henstridge, Som
Ireby Grange, Ireby, Cul
Iridge Place, Hurst Green, Ssx
Irnham Hall, Irnham, Lin
Irton Hall, Irton, Cul
Isel Hall, Isel, Cul
Isenhurst Park, Mayfield, Ssx
Isle (The), Bicton, Sal
Islington Hall, Tilney, Nfk
Itton Court, Itton, Mon
Ivers, Marnhull, Dor
Iwerne Minster House, Iwerne Minster, Dor
Ixworth Abbey, Ixworth, Sfk

Jaques Hall, Bradfield, Ess
Jayes Park, Ockley, Sry

Jaynes Court, Bisley with Lypiatt, Gls
Jervaulx Abbey, East Witton, Yks
Jodrell Hall, Twemlow, Chs
Johnby Hall, Johnby, Cul
Johnson Hall, Eccleshall, Sts
Jordans, Ashill, Som
Joyce Grove, Nettlebed, Oxf
Justicetown, Blackford, Cul

Kedleston Hall, Kedleston, Dby
Keele Hall, Keele, Sts
Keep Hatch, Wokingham, Brk
Keevil Manor House, Keevil, Wil
Keldholme Priory, Kirby Moorside, Yks
Keldy Castle, Cropton, Yks
Kellet House, Whicham, Cul
Kelmarsh Hall, Kelmarsh, Nth
Kelston Park, Kelston, Som
Kemble House, Kemble, Gls
Kempston Bury, Kempston, Bdf
Kempston Grange, Kempston, Bdf
Kempston Manor, Kempston, Bdf
Ken Hill, Snettisham, Nfk
Ken Wood, Highgate, Mdx
Kenfield Hall, Petham, Ken
Kennett Hall, Kennett, Cam
Kensington Palace, Kensington, Mdx
Kenswick, Kenswick, Wor
Kent House, Hammersmith, Mdx
Kentchurch Court, Kentchurch, Hef
Kentwell Hall, Long Melford, Sfk
Kenward, Yalding, Ken
Kenwick Hall, Legbourne, Lin
Kenwith Castle, Abbotsham, Dev
Kenyon Hall, Little Hulton, Lan
Kepwick Hall, Over Silton, Yks
Keresley Grange, Keresley and Coundon, War
Kermincham Lodge, Kermincham, Chs
Keswick Hall, Keswick, Nfk
Ketteringham Park, Ketteringham, Nfk
Kettlethorpe Hall, Crigglestone, Yks
Kevington, St Mary Cray, Ken
Keythorpe Grange, East Norton, Lei
Keythorpe Hall, Tugby, Lei
Kibblestone Hall, Oulton, Sts
Kiddington Hall, Kiddington, Oxf
Kielder Castle, Falstone, Nbl
Kiftsgate House, Mickleton, Gls
Kilbourne Hall, Kilbourne, Dby
Kildale Hall, Kildale, Yks
Kildwick Hall, Kildwick, Yks
Killagorden, St Clement, Con
Killerby Hall, Cayton, Yks
Killerton, Broadclyst, Dev
Killhow, Boltons, Cul
Killiganoon, St Feock, Con
Killingholme Manor, North Killingholme, Lin
Killiow, Kea, Con
Kilnwick Percy Hall, Kilnwick Percy, Yks
Kilve Court, Kilve, Som

Kilverstone Hall, Kilverstone, Nfk
Kilvington Hall, Thornton le Street, Yks
Kilworth House, North Kilworth, Lei
Kilworthy House, Tavistock, Dev
Kimberley House, Carleton Forehoe, Nfk
Kimbolton Castle, Kimbolton, Hun
Kimpton Lodge, Kimpton, Ham
Kimsbury, Upton St Leonards, Gls
Kineton House, Kineton, War
King's Ford, Stanway All Saints, Ess
King's Nympton Park, King's Nympton, Dev
King's Sutton Manor House, King's Sutton, Nth
King's Weston House, Henbury, Gls
Kingerby Hall, Kingerby, Lin
Kingfield House, Nichol Forest, Cul
Kings Walden Bury, Kings Walden, Hrt
Kingscote Park, Kingscote, Gls
Kingsdown House, Kingsdown near Deal, Ken
Kingsdown House, Stratton St Margaret, Wil
Kingsmead, Matfield, Ken
Kingsthorpe Hall, Northampton, Nth
Kingston Hall, Kingston on Soar, Ntt
Kingston House, Aston Rowant, Oxf
Kingston House, Kingston Bagpuize, Brk
Kingston House, Staverton, Dev
Kingston Lacy, Pamphill, Dor
Kingston Lisle Park, Kingston Lisle, Brk
Kingston Maurward, Stinsford, Dor
Kingswear Castle, Kingswear, Dev
Kingthorpe, Pickering, Yks
Kinlet Hall, Kinlet, Sal
Kinnersley Castle, Kinnersley, Hef
Kinnersley Manor, Horley, Sry
Kinsham Court, Kinsham, Hef
Kinwarton House, Kinwarton, War
Kiplin Hall, Bolton upon Swale, Yks
Kippax Park, Kippax, Yks
Kirby Cane Hall, Kirby Cane, Nfk
Kirby House, Inkpen, Brk
Kirby Misperton Hall, Kirby Misperton, Yks
Kirk Hammerton Hall, Kirk Hammerton, Yks
Kirkby Hall, Kirkby Fleetham, Yks
Kirkby Mallory Hall, Kirkby Mallory, Lei
Kirkdale Manor, Kirkdale, Yks
Kirkham Hall, Kirkham, Yks
Kirkleatham Hall, Kirkleatham, Yks
Kirklees Hall, Clifton, Yks
Kirkley Hall, Ponteland, Nbl
Kirklington Hall, Kirklington, Ntt
Kirklington Hall, Kirklington, Yks
Kirklinton Hall, Kirklinton, Cul
Kirklinton Park, Kirklinton, Cul
Kirtling Tower, Kirtling, Cam
Kirtlington Park, Kirtlington, Oxf
Kitemore, Shellingford, Brk
Kitley, Yealmpton, Dev
Kitwells, Ridge, Hrt
Knapton Hall, Knapton, Yks
Knapton House, Knapton, Nfk
Knebworth House, Knebworth, Hrt

Knedlington Manor, Howden, Yks
Kneesworth Hall, Bassingbourn, Cam
Knells (The), Houghton, Cul
Knepp Castle, Shipley, Ssx
Knightley Grange, Gnosall, Sts
Knighton, Durweston, Dor
Knightshayes Court, Tiverton, Dev
Knill Court, Knill, Hef
Knockin Hall, Knockin, Sal
Knole Park, Almondsbury, Gls
Knole, Sevenoaks, Ken
Knolls, Leighton Buzzard, Bdf
Knossington Grange, Knossington, Lei
Knowle, Clyst St George, Dev
Knowle, Cranleigh, Sry
Knowle, Frant, Ssx
Knowle Hall, Bawdrip, Som
Knowle Hall, Knowle, War
Knowle (The), Brenchley, Ken
Knowle, Timberscombe, Som
Knowlemere Manor, Slaidburn, Yks
Knowlton Court, Knowlton, Ken
Knowsley Hall, Knowsley, Lan
Knuston Hall, Irchester, Nth
Kyneton House, Thornbury, Gls
Kyre Park, Kyre Wyard, Wor

Lackford Manor House, Lackford, Sfk
Lackham House, Lacock, Wil
Lacock Abbey, Lacock, Wil
Ladham House, Goudhurst, Ken
Ladstock, Thornthwaite, Cul
Lady Cross Lodge, Boldre, Ham
La Hague Manor, St Peter, Jersey
Lainston House, Sparsholt, Ham
Lairbeck, Keswick, Cul
Lairthwaite, Keswick, Cul
Laithes (The), Laithes, Cul
Lakers Lodge, Loxwood, Ssx
Lambeth Palace, Lambeth, Sry
Lambton Castle, Burnmoor, Dur
Lamellen, St Tudy, Con
Lamer Park, Wheathampstead, Hrt
La Moye House, St Brelade, Jersey
Lanarth, St Keverne, Con
Landford Manor, Landford, Wil
Landing (The), Finsthwaite, Lan
Landue, Lezant, Con
Landwades Hall, Moulton, Sfk
Lane (The), Newbiggin on Lune, Wes
Langcliffe Hall, Langcliffe, Yks
Langdon Court, Wembury, Dev
Langdon House, Dawlish, Dev
Langdown, Dibden, Ham
Langford Court, Burrington, Som
Langford Hall, Langford, Ntt
Langford House, Churchill, Som
Langford Manor, Fivehead, Som
Langhale House, Kirstead, Nfk
Langham Hall, Langham, Ess

Langham Hall, Langham, Sfk
Langley Castle, Hexham, Nbl
Langley Hall, Kirk Langley, Dby
Langley Hall, Langley, Nfk
Langley House, Langley, Wil
Langley House, Slough, Bkm
Langley Manor, Colbury, Ham
Langley Park, Langley Marish, Bkm
Langley Priory, Langley Priory, Lei
Langleybury, Langleybury, Hrt
Langleys, Great Waltham, Ess
Langrish House, Langrish, Ham
Langston House, Chadlington, Oxf
Langstone Court, Llangarron, Hef
Langton Grange, Darlington, Dur
Langton Hall, Langton by Spilsby, Lin
Langton Hall, Langton, Yks
Langton Hall, Little Langton, Yks
Langton Hall, West Langton, Lei
Langton House, Langton, Dor
Lanhydrock House, Lanhydrock, Con
Lanwithan, St Winnow, Con
Larches (The), Ashton, Lan
Lartington Hall, Romaldkirk, Yks
Lasborough Park, Newington Bagpath, Gls
Lathom House, Lathom, Lan
Latimer House, Latimer, Bkm
Lattenbury Hill, Papworth St Agnes, Cam
Lauderdale House, Highgate, Mdx
Launde Abbey, Launde, Lei
Lavant House, Lavant, Ssx
Lavenham Hall, Lavenham, Sfk
Laverstoke House, Laverstoke, Ham
Lavethan, Blisland, Con
Lavington Park, Woolavington, Ssx
Lawford Hall, Lawford, Ess
Lawkland Hall, Austwick, Yks
Lawn House, Hampstead, Mdx
Lawn (The), Swindon, Wil
Lawrence End, Kimpton, Hrt
Layton Manor, Hutton Magna, Yks
Lazonby Hall, Lazonby, Cul
Lea Castle, Wolverley, Wor
Lea Green, Lea, Dby
Lea Hall, Lea, Lin
Lea Hall, Preston Gubbals, Sal
Lea Hurst, Holloway, Dby
Lea (The), Adbaston, Sts
Leadenham House, Leadenham, Lin
Leagram Hall, Little Bowland, Lan
Leases Hall, Bedale, Yks
Leaton Hall, Bobbington, Sts
Leaton Knolls, Leaton, Sal
Leawood, Bridestowe, Dev
Leazes, Hexham, Nbl
Lechlade Manor House, Lechlade, Gls
Leck Hall, Leck, Lan
Leckford Abbess, Leckford, Ham
Leckhampton Court, Leckhampton, Gls
Le Court, Greatham, Ham

Ledgers, Chelsham, Sry
Ledston Hall, Ledston, Yks
Lee Ford, Budleigh Salterton, Dev
Lee Hall, Bellingham, Nbl
Lee Manor House, Lee, Ken
Lee Place, Charlbury, Oxf
Lee Priory, Ickham, Ken
Leeds Castle, Leeds, Ken
Leeming Garth, Bedale, Yks
Lees Court, Sheldwich, Ken
Leesthorpe Hall, Leesthorpe, Lei
Leet Hill, Kirby Cane, Nfk
Leez Priory, Little Leighs, Ess
Legbourne Abbey, Legbourne, Lin
Leggatts, Little Heath, Hrt
Leicester Grange, Wolvey, War
Leigh Court, Angersleigh, Som
Leigh House, Winsham, Som
Leigh Manor, Worthen, Sal
Leigh Park, Havant, Ham
Leigham Manor, Egg Buckland, Dev
Leighton Hall, Leighton, Sal
Leiston Old Abbey, Leiston, Sfk
Leith Hill Place, Wotton, Sry
Lemmington Hall, Alnwick, Nbl
Leonardslee, Lower Beeding, Ssx
Les Fontenelles, Forest, Guernsey
Les Granges Manor, St Peter Port, Guernsey
Letcombe Manor, Letcombe, Brk
Letton Court, Letton, Hef
Letton Hall, Letton, Nfk
Le Vallon, St Martin, Guernsey
Levens Hall, Levens, Wes
Lew House, Lewtrenchard, Dev
Lewarne, St Neot, Con
Lewcombe Manor, East Chelborough, Dor
Lewell Lodge, Knighton West, Dor
Leweston Manor, Lillington, Dor
Lexden Park, Colchester, Ess
Lexham Hall, East Lexham, Nfk
Leydene, East Meon, Ham
Leygore Manor, Turkdean, Gls
Liddington Manor, Liddington, Wil
Lifton Park, Lifton, Dev
Light Oaks, Oakamoor, Sts
Lilburn Tower, Alnwick, Nbl
Lilford Hall, Lilford, Nth
Lilies, Weedon, Bkm
Lillingstone House, Lillingstone Dayrell, Bkm
Lillingstone Lovell Manor, Lillingstone Lovell, Bkm
Lily Hill, Bracknell, Brk
Limes (The), Mickleover, Dby
Limes (The), Rushmere St Andrew, Sfk
Lincoln Hill House, Ross, Hef
Lincoln Old Palace, Lincoln, Lin
Linden Hall, Long Horsley, Nbl
Lindridge, Bishopsteignton, Dev
Lindsey House, Blackheath, Ken
Linford Hall, Little Linford, Bkm
Lingcroft, Naburn, Yks

Lingholm, Crosthwaite, Cul
Linley Hall, More, Sal
Linton Park, Linton, Ken
Liscombe Park, Soulbury, Bkm
Litchborough Hall, Litchborough, Nth
Little Aston Hall, Little Aston, Sts
Little Bardfield Hall, Little Bardfield, Ess
Little Barford House, Little Barford, Bdf
Little Bray House, Charles, Dev
Little Compton Manor House, Little Compton, War
Little Dene, Beddingham, Ssx
Little Down House, Holdenhurst, Ham
Little Durnford Manor, Durnford, Wil
Little Grimsby Hall, Little Grimsby, Lin
Little Hadham Place, Little Hadham, Hrt
Little Harle Tower, Kirkharle, Nbl
Little Haugh, Norton, Sfk
Little Hockham, Hockham, Nfk
Little Houghton House, Little Houghton, Nth
Little Marlow Manor House, Little Marlow, Bkm
Little Onn Hall, Church Eaton, Sts
Little Park End, Simonburn, Nbl
Little Park House, Thatcham, Brk
Little Park, Wickham, Ham
Little Plumstead Hall, Little Plumstead, Nfk
Little Ponton Hall, Little Ponton, Lin
Little Rissington Manor House, Little Rissington, Gls
Little Silver, High Bickington, Dev
Little Tew Grange, Little Tew, Oxf
Little Thakeham, Thakeham, Ssx
Little Thurlow Hall, Little Thurlow, Sfk
Little Wyrley Hall, Norton Canes, Sts
Littlecote Park, Ramsbury, Wil
Littledale Hall, Caton, Lan
Littleton Hall, Littleton, Chs
Livermere Hall, Great Livermere, Sfk
Llan-yr-Avon, Llanfrechfa Lower, Mon
Llanarth Court, Llanarth, Mon
Llanforda, Oswestry, Sal
Llangibby Castle, Llangibby, Mon
Llanover House, Llanover, Mon
Llanrumney Hall, St Mellons, Mon
Llantarnam Abbey, Llanvihangel Llantarnam, Mon
Llanvair Grange, Llanvair-Kilgidin, Mon
Llanvihangel Court, Llanvihangel Crucorney, Mon
Llanwenarth House, Llanwenarth Ultra, Mon
Llanwern, Llanwern, Mon
Llwyndu Court, Abergavenny, Mon
Lock, Ashurst, Ssx
Lockeridge House, West Overton, Wil
Lockerley Hall, East Tytherley, Ham
Lockinge House, East Lockinge, Brk
Lockington Hall, Lockington, Lei
Locko Park, Spondon, Dby
Locksley Hall, North Somercotes, Lin
Loddenham Manor, Staplehurst, Ken
Loddington Hall, Loddington, Lei
Loddington Hall, Loddington, Nth
Loddon Court, Swallowfield, Brk
Loders Court, Loders, Dor

Lodge (The), East Bergholt, Sfk
Lodge (The), Richard's Castle, Sal
Lodge (The), Sandy, Bdf
Lodge (The), Weston super Mare, Som
Lodsworth House, Lodsworth, Ssx
Londesborough Park, Londesborough, Yks
Longcroft Hall, Yoxall, Sts
Longcross House, Chertsey, Sry
Longden Manor, Longden, Sal
Longdon Hall, Longdon, Wor
Longford Castle, Britford, Wil
Longford Hall, Longford, Dby
Longford Hall, Longford, Sal
Longfords, Minchinhampton, Gls
Longhills, Branston and Mere, Lin
Longhirst Hall, Longhirst, Nbl
Longleat, Longbridge Deverill, Wil
Longner Hall, Atcham, Sal
Longnor Hall, Longnor, Sal
Longparish House, Longparish, Ham
Longstock Park, Longstock, Ham
Longstowe Hall, Longstowe, Cam
Longthorns, Milborne St Andrew, Dor
Longueville Manor, St Saviour, Jersey
Longwitton Hall, Hartburn, Nbl
Longwood House, Owslebury, Ham
Longworth Hall, Lugwardine, Hef
Longworth House, Longworth, Brk
Loose Court, Loose, Ken
Loppington House, Loppington, Sal
Lorbottle Hall, Whittingham, Nbl
Lord Chancellor's House, Eltham, Ken
Lordship (The), Benington, Hrt
Lordship (The), Much Hadham, Hrt
Lorton Hall, Lorton, Cul
Lorton House, Broadway, Dor
Loseley Park, Guildford, Sry
Lostock Hall, Bamber Bridge, Lan
Lotherton Hall, Aberford, Yks
Loton Park, Alberbury, Sal
Loudham Hall, Pettistree, Sfk
Loughrigg Brow, Rydal and Loughrigg, Wes
Louis Weedon House, Weedon Lois, Nth
Lovells Court, Marnhull, Dor
Low Bridge House, Selside, Wes
Low Burton Hall, Masham, Yks
Low House, Cotehill, Cul
Low Stakesby, Whitby, Yks
Lower Cousley Wood, Wadhurst, Ssx
Lower Eaton, Eaton Bishop, Hef
Lower Hall, Worfield, Sal
Lower Hare Park, Dullingham, Cam
Lower Hill, Wick, Wor
Lowesby Hall, Lowesby, Lei
Lowlynn House, Kyloe, Nbl
Lowther Castle, Lowther, Wes
Lowthorpe Lodge, Lowthorpe, Yks
Loxley Hall, Loxley, Sts
Loxwood House, Loxwood, Ssx
Loynton Hall, Norbury, Sts

Lucan House, Sharow, Yks
Luddington House, Egham, Sry
Ludford Park, Ludford, Sal
Ludstone Hall, Claverley, Sal
Lufton Manor, Lufton, Som
Lukesland, Harford, Dev
Lullingstone Castle, Lullingstone, Ken
Lulworth Castle, East Lulworth, Dor
Lumley Castle, Lumley, Dur
Lunefield, Kirkby Lonsdale, Wes
Luscombe Castle, Dawlish, Dev
Luton Hoo, Hyde, Bdf
Lutwyche Hall, Rushbury, Sal
Lydham Manor, Lydham, Sal
Lydiard Park, Lydiard Tregoze, Wil
Lydney Park, Lydney, Gls
Lyegrove, Old Sodbury, Gls
Lyme Park, Lyme Handley, Chs
Lyminster House, Lyminster, Ssx
Lymm Hall, Lymm, Chs
Lympne Castle, Lympne, Ken
Lympsham Manor, Lympsham, Som
Lyndenhurst, Dulwich, Sry
Lyndon Hall, Lyndon, Rut
Lyne, Capel, Sry
Lynhales, Lyonshall, Hef
Lynsted Park, Lynsted, Ken
Lynwick, Rudgwick, Ssx
Lypiatt Park, Bisley with Lypiatt, Gls
Lyston Court, Llanwarne, Hef
Lytchett Heath, Lytchett Matravers, Dor
Lytes Cary, Charlton Mackrell, Som
Lyth (The), Ellesmere, Sal
Lytham Hall, Lytham, Lan
Lythe Hill, Haslemere, Sry
Lyulphs Tower, Watermillock, Cul
Lyzwick Hall, Underskiddaw, Cul

Mabledon Park, Tonbridge, Ken
Mablethorpe Hall, Mablethorpe St Mary, Lin
Macartney House, Greenwich, Ken
Madingley Hall, Madingley, Cam
Madresfield Court, Madresfield, Wor
Maer Hall, Maer, Sts
Maidenstone, Bursledon, Ham
Maincombe, West Crewkerne, Som
Mainsforth Hall, Mainsforth, Dur
Mainstone Court, Pixley, Hef
Maisemore Park, Maisemore, Gls
Malham Tarn Hall, Kirkby in Malham Dale, Yks
Mallard's Court, Stokenchurch, Bkm
Malquoits, Ewhurst, Sry
Malshanger, Church Oakley, Ham
Malton Lodge, Malton, Yks
Malverleys, East Woodhay, Ham
Malwood, Minstead, Ham
Mamhead Park, Mamhead, Dev
Mancetter Manor, Mancetter, War
Manley Hall, Manley, Chs
Mannington Hall, Mannington, Nfk

Manor House, Ashby Folville, Lei
Manor House, Barkham, Brk
Manor House, Bishops Hull, Som
Manor House, Brant Broughton and Stragglethorpe, Lin
Manor House, Broughton Gifford, Wil
Manor House, Buriton, Ham
Manor House, Costock, Ntt
Manor House, Dinsdale, Dur
Manor House, Dowles, Wor
Manor House, Farrington Gurney, Som
Manor House, Fifehead Neville, Dor
Manor House, Greatham, Ham
Manor House, Greenwich, Ken
Manor House, Hackney, Mdx
Manor House, Hazelbury Bryan, Dor
Manor House, Holcombe, Som
Manor House, Little Berkhamsted, Hrt
Manor House, Mells, Som
Manor House, Middleton Tyas, Yks
Manor House, Minstead, Ham
Manor House, Morebath, Dev
Manor House, Morpeth, Nbl
Manor House, Normanton on Soar, Ntt
Manor House, Ottery St Mary, Dev
Manor House, Princes Risborough, Bkm
Manor House, Stone, Wor
Manor House, Stratton Audley, Oxf
Manor House, Swanbourne, Bkm
Manor House (The), Bosham, Ssx
Manor House (The), Chadlington, Oxf
Manor House (The), Cliffe Pypard, Wil
Manor House (The), Corfe Castle, Dor
Manor House (The), Hemingford Grey, Hun
Manor House (The), Kilmington, Wil
Manor House (The), Lee, Bkm
Manor House (The), Stinchcombe, Gls
Manor House (The), Sutton Courtenay, Brk
Manor House (The), Thorpe Mandeville, Nth
Manor House (The), Trent, Dor
Manor House (The), Upton Grey, Ham
Manor House (The), Walton, Bkm
Manor House (The), West Haddon, Nth
Manor House (The), Yattendon, Brk
Manor House, Tockenham, Wil
Manor House, Welbourn, Lin
Manor House, West Deeping, Lin
Manor House, Yarnton, Oxf
Manor (The), Carlton Scroop, Lin
Manor (The), Drayton, Brk
Manor (The), Long Crendon, Bkm
Manor (The), Sidmouth, Dev
Manor (The), Temple Sowerby, Wes
Manresa House, Putney, Sry
Mansion House, St Mary Woolchurch, Lnd
Manston House, Manston, Dor
Manydown Park, Wootton St Lawrence, Ham
Maperton House, Maperton, Som
Maple hayes, Burntwood, Sts
Mapledurham House, Mapledurham, Oxf
Mapleton, Four Elms, Ken

INDEX OF ENGLISH COUNTRY HOUSES

Maplewell Hall, Woodhouse Eaves, Lei
Mapperton House, Mapperton, Dor
Marbury Hall, Marbury, Chs
Marbury Hall, Marbury cum Quoisley, Chs
Marcham Park, Marcham, Brk
Marche Hall, Westbury, Sal
Marchwood Park, Marchwood, Ham
Marden Hill, Tewin, Hrt
Marden Park, Woldingham, Sry
Margery Hall, Ewell, Sry
Marham House, Marham, Nfk
Maristow, Tamerton Foliot, Dev
Mark Hall, Latton, Ess
Markly, Warbleton, Ssx
Marks Hall, Markshall, Ess
Markyate Cell, Markyate, Hrt
Marlesford Hall, Marlesford, Sfk
Marlingford Hall, Marlingford, Nfk
Marlow Place, Marlow, Bkm
Marlston House, Marlston, Brk
Marrington Hall, Chirbury, Sal
Marshchapel Hall, Marshchapel, Lin
Marske Hall, Marske by the Sea, Yks
Marske Hall, Marske, Yks
Marston Hill, Marston Maisey, Wil
Marston Manor House, Marston St Lawrence, Nth
Marston Park, Marston Bigot, Som
Marston Trussell Hall, Marston Trussell, Nth
Martley Hall, Easton, Sfk
Marton Hall, Myddle, Sal
Marton House, Long Marton, Wes
Marwell Hall, Owslebury, Ham
Matcham, Hurn, Ham
Matfen Hall, Matfen, Nbl
Maugersbury Manor, Stow on the Wold, Gls
Maunby Hall, Kirby Wiske, Yks
Maunsell Grange, St Michael Church, Som
Mawley Hall, Cleobury Mortimer, Sal
Maxstoke Castle, Maxstoke, War
Meaford Hall, Meaford, Sts
Mears Ashby Hall, Mears Ashby, Nth
Medmenham Abbey, Medmenham, Bkm
Meesden Manor, Meesden, Hrt
Meeson Hall, Bolas Magna, Sal
Melbourne Hall, Melbourne, Dby
Melbourne Hall, Thornton, Yks
Melbury House, Melbury Sampford, Dor
Melchbourne Park, Melchbourne, Bdf
Melchet Court, Melchet Park, Ham
Meldon Park, Meldon, Nbl
Melford Hall, Long Melford, Sfk
Melford Place, Long Melford, Sfk
Mellifont Abbey, Wookey, Som
Mells Park, Mells, Som
Melmerby Hall, Melmerby, Cul
Melmerby Hall, Wath, Yks
Melplash Court, Melplash, Dor
Melton Constable Hall, Melton Constable, Nfk
Menabilly, Tywardreath, Con
Mendip Lodge, Churchill, Som

Menehay House, Budock, Con
Menethorpe Hall, Westow, Yks
Mentmore, Mentmore, Bkm
Mere Hall, Hanbury, Wor
Mere Hall, Mere, Chs
Mere New Hall, Mere, Chs
Meredith, Tibberton, Gls
Merevale Hall, Merevale, War
Mereworth Castle, Mereworth, Ken
Mergate Hall, Bracon Ash, Nfk
Meriden Hall, Meriden, War
Meriden House, Meriden, War
Merly House, Canford Magna, Dor
Mersham le Hatch, Mersham, Ken
Merstham House, Merstham, Sry
Merton Hall, Merton, Nfk
Messing Park, Messing, Ess
Metham Hall, Laxton, Yks
Methley Hall, Methley, Yks
Mettingham Castle, Mettingham, Sfk
Meynell Langley, Kirk Langley, Dby
Michaelchurch Court, Michaelchurch Eskley, Hef
Michaelstow Hall, Ramsey, Ess
Michaelstow House, Michaelstow, Con
Michelham Priory, Chiddingly, Ssx
Mickleton Manor, Mickleton, Gls
Middle Hill, Broadway, Wor
Middlecot, Amport, Ham
Middleton Hall, Belford, Nbl
Middleton Hall, Ilderton, Nbl
Middleton Hall, Middleton, Dby
Middleton Hall, Middleton, Nfk
Middleton Hall, Middleton, War
Middleton House, Longparish, Ham
Middleton Lodge, Middleton Tyas, Yks
Middleton Park, Middleton Stoney, Oxf
Middleton Tower, Middleton, Nfk
Middleton, Westmeston, Ssx
Middlewich Manor House, Newton by Middlewich, Chs
Midelney Place, Drayton, Som
Midgham House, Midgham, Brk
Milbourne Hall, Ponteland, Nbl
Mildenhall Manor House, Mildenhall, Sfk
Mileham Hall, Mileham, Nfk
Milfield, Kirknewton, Nbl
Milford Hall, Baswich, Sts
Milgate Park, Thurnham, Ken
Mill Hill, Brandsby, Yks
Mill House, Dersingham, Nfk
Mill House, North Mundham, Ssx
Milland Place, Milland, Ssx
Millaton, Bridestowe, Dev
Millholme, Bootle, Cul
Millichope Park, Munslow, Sal
Milner Field, Bingley, Yks
Milton Abbey, Milton Abbas, Dor
Milton Court, Dorking, Sry
Milton Ernest Hall, Milton Ernest, Bdf
Milton Hall, Castor, Nth
Milton Heath, Dorking, Sry

Milton Hill, Milton, Brk
Milton House, Milton, Brk
Milton Lodge, Wells, Som
Milton Manor, Milton, Nth
Milton Park, Egham, Sry
Milton Priory, Great Milton, Oxf
Minley Manor, Minley, Ham
Minstead Lodge, Minstead, Ham
Minster Abbey, Minster, Ken
Minster Acres Hall, Healey St John, Nbl
Minterne House, Minterne Magna, Dor
Mirehouse, Bassenthwaite, Cul
Miserden Park, Miserden, Gls
Missenden Abbey, Great Missenden, Bkm
Missenden House, Little Missenden, Bkm
Misterton Hall, Misterton, Lei
Mitford Hall, Mitford, Nbl
Moat (The), Ipswich, Sfk
Moatlands, Brenchley, Ken
Mobberley Hall, Mobberley, Chs
Mobberley Manor House, Mobberley, Chs
Mobberley Old Hall, Mobberley, Chs
Moccas Court, Moccas, Hef
Moditonham, Botus Fleming, Con
Moigne Combe, Owermoigne, Dor
Molecomb, Singleton, Ssx
Mollington Hall, Mollington, Chs
Mongewell Park, Mongewell, Oxf
Monk Coniston Park, Coniston, Lan
Monk Fryston Hall, Monk Fryston, Yks
Monkhams Hall, Waltham Abbey, Ess
Monkhopton House, Monkhopton, Sal
Monks Horton Park, Monks Horton, Ken
Monks Park, Corsham, Wil
Monkshatch, Compton, Sry
Monkton Farleigh Manor House, Monkton Farleigh,
  Wil
Montacute House, Montacute, Som
Montreal, Riverhead, Ken
Moor Court, Amberley, Gls
Moor Court, Oakamoor, Sts
Moor Court, Pembridge, Hef
Moor Hall, Harlow, Ess
Moor Park, Beckwithshaw, Yks
Moor Park, Farnham, Sry
Moor Park, Richard's Castle, Sal
Moor Place, Much Hadham, Hrt
Moor (The), Clifford, Hef
Moor (The), Stoke St Milborough, Sal
Moore Hall, Moore, Chs
Moore House, Moore, Chs
Moorlands, Merriott, Som
Moors (The), Birlingham, Wor
Moortown House, South Kelsey, Lin
Moorwood House, Bagendon, Gls
Morant's Court, Chevening, Ken
Moraston House, Bridstow, Hef
Morcott Hall, Morcott, Rut
Moreby Hall, Stillingfleet, Yks
Morecambe Lodge, Yealand Conyers, Lan

Moredon, North Curry, Som
Moresdale Hall, Lambrigg, Wes
Moreton, Bideford, Dev
Moreton Court, Moreton on Lugg, Hef
Moreton Hall, Moreton Morrell, War
Moreton Hall, Whalley, Lan
Moreton House, Moreton, Dor
Moreton Paddox, Moreton Morrell, War
Morland Hall, Morland, Wes
Morley Hall, Morley St Peter, Nfk
Morningthorpe Manor, Morningthorpe, Nfk
Mortimer Hill, Stratfield Mortimer, Brk
Mortimer House, Stratfield Mortimer, Brk
Mortimer Lodge, Stratfield Mortimer, Brk
Morton Hall, Babworth, Ntt
Morton Hall, Morton by Lincoln, Lin
Morton Hall, Morton, Nfk
Morval House, Morval, Con
Mosborough Hall, Mosborough, Dby
Mosborough Hill House, Mosborough, Dby
Moseley Court, Bushbury, Sts
Moston Hall, Moston, Chs
Motcombe House, Motcombe, Dor
Mottisfont Abbey, Mottisfont, Ham
Mottram Hall, Mottram St Andrew, Chs
Moulton Grange, Moulton, Nth
Moulton Hall, Middleton Tyas, Yks
Moulton Paddocks, Moulton, Sfk
Moundsley Hall, Wythall, Wor
Mount Clare, Putney, Sry
Mount Edgcumbe, Maker, Con
Mount Sion, Selattyn, Sal
Mount St John, Felixkirk, Yks
Mount (The), Ifield, Ssx
Mount (The), Tettenhall, Sts
Mountfield Court, Mountfield, Ssx
Mowbray House, Kirkby Malzeard, Yks
Mowbreck Hall, Medlar, Lan
Moxhull Hall, Wishaw, War
Moyles Court, Ellingham, Ham
Moynes Court, Mathern, Mon
Moyns Park, Steeple Bumpstead, Ess
Mulgrave Castle, Lythe, Yks
Muncaster Castle, Muncaster, Cul
Munden, Leavesden, Hrt
Munderfield Harold, Bromyard, Hef
Muntham Court, Findon, Ssx
Mursley Hall, Mursley, Bkm
Myddelton House, Enfield, Mdx
Mynde Park, Much Dewchurch, Hef
Mystole Park, Chartham, Ken
Myton Hall, Myton upon Swale, Yks

Naburn Hall, Naburn, Yks
Nailcote Hall, Berkswell, War
Naish Priory, East Coker, Som
Nancealverne, Madron, Con
Nanpantan Hall, Nanpantan, Lei
Nansloe, Wendron, Con
Nant Oer, Abergavenny, Mon

Narborough Hall, Narborough, Nfk
Narborough House, Narborough, Nfk
Narford Hall, Narford, Nfk
Naseby Hall, Naseby, Nth
Nash Court, Boughton, Ken
Nash Court, Burford, Sal
Nash Court, Marnhull, Dor
Nateby Lodge, Nateby, Lan
Naworth Castle, Naworth, Cul
Nawton Tower, Kirkdale, Yks
Nazeing Park, Nazeing, Ess
Neach Hill, Donington, Sal
Neasham Abbey, Darlington, Dur
Neasham Hall, Darlington, Dur
Neaum Crag, Rydal and Loughrigg, Wes
Necton Hall, Necton, Nfk
Nedging Grange, Nedging, Sfk
Needham Hall, Friday Bridge, Cam
Needwood House, Rolleston, Sts
Neston Park, Neston, Wil
Neswick Hall, Bainton, Yks
Nether Hall, Hathersage, Dby
Nether Hall, Pakenham, Sfk
Nether Swell Manor, Nether Swell, Gls
Nether Warden, Warden, Nbl
Nether Winchendon Manor, Nether Winchendon, Bkm
Netherby Hall, Netherby, Cul
Nethercott, Iddesleigh, Dev
Netherfield, Stanstead Abbotts, Hrt
Nethergrove, High Bickington, Dev
Netherhall, Maryport, Cul
Netherlea, Holbrook, Dby
Netherside Hall, Linton, Yks
Netherton Hall, Farway, Dev
Nethway House, Brixham and Kingswear, Dev
Netley Castle, Netley Abbey, Ham
Netley Hall, Stapleton, Sal
Netley Park, Shere, Sry
Nettlecombe Court, Nettlecombe, Som
Nettleham Hall, Nettleham, Lin
Nettleworth Manor, Sookholme, Ntt
New Grove House, Hampstead, Mdx
New Moreton Hall, Astbury, Chs
New Park, Brockenhurst, Ham
New Place, Porlock, Som
New Place, Shedfield, Ham
Newark Park, Ozleworth, Gls
Newbiggin Hall, Blanchland, Nbl
Newbiggin Hall, Brisco, Cul
Newbiggin Hall, Newbiggin, Wes
Newbiggin House, Whitley near Hexham, Nbl
Newbold Pacey Hall, Newbold Pacey, War
Newbottle Manor House, Newbottle, Nth
Newbrough Park, Newbrough, Nbl
Newbuilding, Kirby Knowle, Yks
Newburgh Priory, Coxwold, Yks
Newbury House, Coleford, Som
Newbus Grange, Darlington, Dur
Newby Grange, Low Crosby, Cul
Newby Hall, Skelton, Yks

Newby Wiske Hall, Kirby Wiske, Yks
Newcombes, Crediton, Dev
Newcourt, Lugwardine, Hef
Newdigate Place, Newdigate, Sry
Newe House, Pakenham, Sfk
Newells, Lower Beeding, Ssx
Newent Court, Newent, Gls
Newhouse, Mersham, Ken
Newhouse, Redlynch, Wil
Newick Park, Newick, Ssx
Newland House, Newland, Gls
Newland Park, Chalfont St Peter, Bkm
Newlands Manor, Milford on Sea, Ham
Newnham Manor, Newnham Murren, Oxf
Newnham Paddox, Monks Kirby, War
Newnham Park, Plympton St Mary, Dev
Newport Towers, Berkeley, Gls
Newsells Park, Barkway, Hrt
Newsham Hall, Winston, Dur
Newtimber Place, Newtimber, Ssx
Newton Court, Dixton, Mon
Newton Ferrers, St Mellion, Con
Newton Hall, Dunmow, Ess
Newton Hall, Newton by Chester, Chs
Newton Hall, Newton, Cam
Newton Hall, Newton Hall, Nbl
Newton Hall, Newton Kyme, Yks
Newton Hall, Newton near Folkingham, Lin
Newton Hall, Shilbottle, Nbl
Newton House, Newton St Cyres, Dev
Newton Low Hall, Shilbottle, Nbl
Newton Manor House, Newton, Cam
Newton Manor, Swanage, Dor
Newton Park, Newton Solney, Dby
Newton Park, Newton St Loe, Som
Newton Surmaville, Yeovil, Som
Newton Valence Manor House, Newton Valence, Ham
Newtown House, Newtown, Ham
Newtown Park, South Baddesley, Ham
Nidd Hall, Nidd, Yks
Noak (The), Martley, Wor
Noake (The), Hucclecote, Gls
Nocton Hall, Nocton, Lin
Node (The), Codicote, Hrt
Noirmont Manor, St Brelade, Jersey
Norbury Booths Hall, Over Knutsford, Chs
Norcliffe Hall, Styal, Chs
Norley Bank, Norley, Chs
Norley Hall, Norley, Chs
Norman Court, West Tytherley, Ham
Norman Hill, Cam, Gls
Normanby Hall, Normanby near Middlesbrough, Yks
Normanby Park, Burton upon Stather, Lin
Normanhurst, Darley Dale, Dby
Normanton Hall, Southwell, Ntt
Norris Castle, East Cowes, Ham
North Aston Hall, North Aston, Oxf
North Carlton Hall, North Carlton, Lin
North Cerney House, North Cerney, Gls
North Clifton Hall, North Clifton, Ntt

North Coker House, East Coker, Som
North Court, Brandon, Sfk
North Cove Hall, North Cove, Sfk
North Frith, Hadlow, Ken
North Grimstone House, North Grimston, Yks
North Mimms Park, North Mimms, Hrt
North Perrott Manor, North Perrott, Som
North Rode Manor House, North Rode, Chs
North Runcton Hall, North Runcton, Nfk
North Runcton Lodge, North Runcton, Nfk
North Walsham Wood, North Walsham, Nfk
Northaw Place, Northaw, Hrt
Northcote Manor, Burrington, Dev
Northcourt, Shorwell, Ham
Northerwood House, Emery Down, Ham
Northgate (The), St Weonards, Hef
Northmoor, Dulverton, Som
Northorpe Hall, Northorpe, Lin
Northrepps Hall, Northrepps, Nfk
Northway House, Ashchurch, Gls
Norton Bavant Manor, Norton Bavant, Wil
Norton Conyers, Wath, Yks
Norton Court, Norton, Gls
Norton Court, Norton, Ken
Norton Disney Hall, Norton Disney, Lin
Norton Grove, Norton, Yks
Norton Hall, Midsomer Norton, Som
Norton Hall, Norton, Nth
Norton Hall, Weston sub Edge, Gls
Norton Manor, Norton Fitzwarren, Som
Norton Place, Bishop Norton, Lin
Norton Priory, Norton Halton, Chs
Norwich Palace, Norwich, Nfk
Norwood Park, Southwell, Ntt
Noseley Hall, Noseley, Lei
Nostell Priory, Wragby, Yks
Nottington House, Radipole, Dor
Notton House, Lacock, Wil
Nowton Court, Nowton, Sfk
Nun Appleton Hall, Appleton Roebuck, Yks
Nuneham Park, Nuneham Courtenay, Oxf
Nunnington Hall, Nunnington, Yks
Nunwell, Brading, Ham
Nunwick Hall, Great Salkeld, Cul
Nunwick Hall, Simonburn, Nbl
Nursery (The), West Felton, Sal
Nurstead Court, Nurstead, Ken
Nursted House, Buriton, Ham
Nutwell Court, Woodbury, Dev
Nymans, Staplefield, Ssx
Nyn Park, Northaw, Hrt
Nynehead Court, Nynehead, Som

Oak Bank, Scotby, Cul
Oak Grove, St Arvans, Mon
Oak Lawn, Hoxne, Sfk
Oak Lodge, Sprowston, Nfk
Oakdown, Burwash, Ssx
Oakes (The), Norton, Dby
Oakfield, Sulhamstead Bannister, Brk

Oakham Lodge, Oakham, Rut
Oakhampton, Astley, Wor
Oakhampton Manor, Wiveliscombe, Som
Oaklands, Dawlish, Dev
Oaklands, Laceby, Lin
Oaklands, Okehampton, Dev
Oaklands Park, Awre, Gls
Oaklands Park, Newdigate, Sry
Oaklands, Sedlescombe, Ssx
Oakley Hall, Deane, Ham
Oakley Hall, Great Oakley, Nth
Oakley Hall, Mucklestone, Sts
Oakley House, Oakley, Bdf
Oakley Manor, Oakley, Ham
Oakly Park, Bromfield, Sal
Oaks (The), North Walsham, Nfk
Oaks (The), Thwaites, Cul
Oakwell House, Birstall, Yks
Oakwood, Funtington, Ssx
Oakwood Hall, Wylam, Nbl
Oare Manor House, Oare, Som
Ockham Park, Ockham, Sry
Ockley Court, Ockley, Sry
Ockwells Manor, Bray, Brk
Ocle Court, Ocle Pychard, Hef
Oddington House, Oddington, Gls
Odell Castle, Odell, Bdf
Offchurch Bury, Offchurch, War
Offley Grove, High Offley, Sts
Offley Place, Offley, Hrt
Offord Cluny Manor House, Offord Cluny, Hun
Offwell House, Offwell, Dev
Ogbeare Hall, North Tamerton, Con
Ogston Hall, Brackenfield, Dby
Okeover Hall, Okeover, Sts
Olands, Milverton, Som
Olantigh, Wye, Ken
Old Alresford House, Old Alresford, Ham
Old Battersea House, Battersea, Sry
Old Blew House, Dulwich, Sry
Old Buckenham Hall, Old Buckenham, Nfk
Old Buckhurst, Withyham, Ssx
Old Castle, Dallington, Ssx
Old Court House, Hampstead, Mdx
Old Dalby Hall, Dalby on the Wolds, Lei
Old Down, Olveston, Gls
Old Grange, Dymock, Gls
Old Grove House, Hampstead, Mdx
Old Hall, Staplefield, Ssx
Old Hall (The), Ellesmere, Sal
Old Hall (The), Oulton, Sts
Old Hill Court, Walford, Hef
Old House, Shipley, Ssx
Old House (The), Aspley Guise, Bdf
Old House (The), Swanbourne, Bkm
Old Manor House, Harrold, Bdf
Old Manor House, Littleton, Mdx
Old Manor, Little Hempston, Dev
Old Manor (The), Moreton Corbet, Sal
Old Mansion (The), Hampstead, Mdx

Old Mansion (The), Henbury, Gls
Old Park, Bosham, Ssx
Old Park, River, Ken
Old Park (The), Axminster, Dev
Old Parsonage, Brenchley, Ken
Old Place, Lindfield, Ssx
Old Possingworth Manor, Waldron, Ssx
Old Sleningford Hall, North Stainley, Yks
Old Springs, Hales, Sts
Old Warden Park, Old Warden, Bdf
Oldbury, Eastington, Gls
Oldbury Hall, Mancetter, War
Oldbury Place, Ightham, Ken
Oldlands Hall, Fairwarp, Ssx
Olive House, Bacup, Lan
Ombersley Court, Ombersley, Wor
Onslow, Bicton, Sal
Orchard Wyndham, Williton, Som
Orchardleigh Park, Orchardleigh, Som
Ord House, Berwick on Tweed, Nbl
Orgreave Hall, Alrewas, Sts
Orleigh Court, Buckland Brewer, Dev
Orleton, Wrockwardine, Sal
Ormerod House, Worsthorne, Lan
Ormesby Hall, Ormesby St Margaret, Nfk
Ormesby Hall, Ormesby, Yks
Ormesby Old Hall, Ormesby St Margaret, Nfk
Ormsby Hall, South Ormsby, Lin
Orpington Priory, Orpington, Ken
Orsett Hall, Orsett, Ess
Orton Hall, Orton Longueville, Hun
Orton Hall, Orton, Wes
Orwell Park, Nacton, Sfk
Osbaston Hall, Osbaston, Lei
Osberton Hall, Osberton, Ntt
Osmaston Manor, Osmaston, Dby
Osmington House, Osmington, Dor
Ossemsley Manor, Milton, Ham
Ossington Hall, Ossington, Ntt
Osterley House, Heston, Mdx
Oswaldkirk Hall, Oswaldkirk, Yks
Oteley, Ellesmere, Sal
Otterburn Dene, Elsdon, Nbl
Otterburn Tower, Elsdon, Nbl
Otterden Place, Otterden, Ken
Otterhead House, Churchstanton, Som
Otterington Hall, South Otterington, Yks
Ouborough, Tandridge, Sry
Oulton Hall, Oulton, Nfk
Oulton Park, Little Budworth, Chs
Ousden Hall, Ousden, Sfk
Outwoods (The), Little Easton, Dby
Over Court, Almondsbury, Gls
Over Norton House, Chipping Norton, Oxf
Overbury Court, Overbury, Wor
Overstrand Hall, Overstrand, Nfk
Overthorpe Hall, Warkworth, Nth
Overton Grange, Richard's Castle, Sal
Overton Hall, Ashover, Dby
Oving House, Oving, Bkm

Ovington Park, Ovington, Ham
Oxborough Hall, Oxborough, Nfk
Oxendon Hall, Great Oxendon, Nth
Oxenways, Membury, Dev
Oxnead Hall, Oxnead, Nfk
Oxon Hoath, West Peckham, Ken
Oxton Hall, Oxton, Ntt
Oxton House, Kenton, Dev
Ozleworth Park, Ozleworth, Gls

Packham House, Fordingbridge, Ham
Packington Hall, Great Packington, War
Packington Hall, Weeford, Sts
Packwood Hall, Packwood, War
Packwood House, Lapworth, War
Padworth House, Padworth, Brk
Pains Hill, Walton on Thames, Sry
Painsthorpe Hall, Kirby Underdale, Yks
Painswick House, Painswick, Gls
Pakenham Lodge, Pakenham, Sfk
Palace House, Beaulieu, Ham
Palace (The), Exeter, Dev
Palace (The), Mathern, Mon
Palace (The), Much Hadham, Hrt
Pallinsburn House, Ford, Nbl
Pampisford Hall, Pampisford, Cam
Panfield Hall, Panfield, Ess
Panshanger, Hertingfordbury, Hrt
Pant-y-goitre, Llanvair-Kilgidin, Mon
Panton Hall, Panton, Lin
Papillon Hall, Lubenham, Lei
Papplewick Grange, Papplewick, Ntt
Papplewick Hall, Papplewick, Ntt
Paradise House, Painswick, Gls
Paragon House, Blackheath, Ken
Parham Hall, Parham, Sfk
Parham Park, Parham, Ssx
Park End, Simonburn, Nbl
Park Hall, Aislaby, Yks
Park Hall, Caverswall, Sts
Park Hall, Hayfield, Dby
Park Hall, Salford Priors, War
Park Hall, Spink Hill, Dby
Park Hall, Warsop, Ntt
Park Hatch, Hascombe, Sry
Park Hill, Firbeck, Yks
Park Hill, Middleton, Nfk
Park Hill, Streatham, Sry
Park House, Boxley, Ken
Park House, Donington, Lin
Park House, Over Stowey, Som
Park Place, Remenham Hill, Brk
Park Place, Wickham, Ham
Park (The), Boxley, Ken
Park (The), Ledbury, Hef
Parke, Bovey Tracey, Dev
Parklands, Shere, Sry
Parklands, Whitminster, Gls
Parmoor, Hambleden, Bkm
Parndon Hall, Little Parndon, Ess

Parnham House, Beaminster, Dor
Parrock's Lodge, Tatworth, Som
Parrox Hall, Preesall, Lan
Part-y-Seal, Grosmont, Mon
Pashley Manor, Ticehurst, Ssx
Passford House, Sway, Ham
Paston Hall, Paston, Nfk
Pasture House, North Otterington, Yks
Patshull House, Patshull, Sts
Patterdale Hall, Patterdale, Wes
Paultons, Copythorne, Ham
Pawston House, Kirknewton, Nbl
Pax Hill Park, Lindfield, Ssx
Paxton Hill House, Great Paxton, Hun
Peak House, Sidmouth, Dev
Peamore, Exminster, Dev
Peatling Hall, Peatling Parva, Lei
Peatswood, Hales, Sts
Peckforton Castle, Peckforton, Chs
Peel Hall, Little Hulton, Lan
Pelhams, Newton Valence, Ham
Pelyn, Lanlivery Rural, Con
Pen Moel, Tidenham, Gls
Penair, St Clement, Con
Pencarrow, Egloshayle, Con
Pencraig Court, Marstow, Hef
Pendarves, Treslothan, Con
Pendrell Hall, Codsall, Sts
Pengersick Castle, Breage, Con
Pengethly, Sellack, Hef
Pengreep, Gwennap, Con
Penhale, Feock, Con
Penheale Manor, Egloskerry, Con
Penjerrick, Budock, Con
Penmount, St Clement, Con
Penn House, Penn Street, Bkm
Pennoxstone Court, King's Caple, Hef
Penns in the Rocks, Withyham, Ssx
Penny Bridge Hall, Egton cum Newland, Lan
Penny Pot, Halstead, Ess
Penquite, St Sampson, Con
Penrice, St Austell, Con
Penrose, Porthleven, Con
Penshurst Place, Penshurst, Ken
Penstowe, Kilkhampton, Con
Pentillie Castle, Pillaton, Con
Penton Lodge, Penton Mewsey, Ham
Pentre-Pant Hall, Hengoed cum Gobowen, Sal
Pentre (The), Abergavenny, Mon
Penwortham Hall, Penwortham, Lan
Penwortham Priory, Penwortham, Lan
Peover Hall, Over Peover, Chs
Peperharow, Peper Harow, Sry
Peplow Hall, Hodnet, Sal
Pepper Arden, South Cowton, Yks
Perceval House, Blackheath, Ken
Perridge House, Pilton, Som
Perrycroft, Colwall, Hef
Perrystone Court, Foy, Hef
Pett Place, Charing, Ken

Petticombe, Monkleigh, Dev
Pettypool House, Weaverham, Chs
Petworth House, Petworth, Ssx
Pickenham Hall, South Pickenham, Nfk
Pickering Hall, Pickering, Yks
Pickforde, Ticehurst, Ssx
Pickhurst House, Chiddingfold
Picts' Hill, Turvey, Bdf
Pierrepont, Frensham, Sry
Pillerton Hersey Manor House, Pillerton Hersey, War
Pilsdon Manor House, Pilsdon, Dor
Pimley Manor, Uffington, Sal
Pinchbeck Hall, Pinchbeck, Lin
Pinchinthorpe Hall, Guisborough, Yks
Pinchinthorpe House, Guisborough, Yks
Pinetoft, Rushmere, Sfk
Pinhay, Axmouth, Dev
Pinkney Park, Sherston, Wil
Pippingford Park, Nutley, Ssx
Pirton Court, Pirton, Wor
Pirton Hall, Pirton, Hrt
Pitchcombe House, Pitchcombe, Gls
Pitchford Hall, Pitchford, Sal
Pitsford Hall, Pitsford, Nth
Pitshill, Tillington, Ssx
Pitt House, Chudleigh Knighton, Dev
Pitt House, Hampstead, Mdx
Pixton Park, Dulverton, Som
Place, Fowey, Con
Place Newton, Wintringham, Yks
Place, St Anthony in Roseland, Con
Plaish Hall, Cardington, Sal
Plashwood, Haughley, Sfk
Plaw Hatch, Bishops Stortford, Hrt
Playford Hall, Playford, Sfk
Playford Mount, Playford, Sfk
Pleasaunce (The), Overstrand, Nfk
Pleasington Hall, Pleasington, Lan
Plowden Hall, Lydbury North, Sal
Plumton House, Whepstead, Sfk
Plush Manor, Buckland Newton, Dor
Pockeridge Park, Corsham, Wil
Pole House, Ide, Dev
Polebrook Hall, Polebrook, Nth
Polesden Lacey, Great Bookham, Sry
Pollards Park, Chalfont St Giles, Bkm
Polstead Hall, Polstead, Sfk
Polwhele, St Clement, Con
Pond House, Dulwich, Sry
Ponsonby Hall, Ponsonby, Cul
Pontrilas Court, Kentchurch, Hef
Poole Hall, Poole, Chs
Pooley Hall, Polesworth, War
Pope's House, Binfield, Brk
Poringland House, Poringland, Nfk
Port Eliot, St Germans, Con
Portal, Tarporley, Chs
Portington Hall, Eastrington, Yks
Portledge, Alwington, Dev
Poslingford House, Poslingford, Sfk

INDEX OF ENGLISH COUNTRY HOUSES

Possingworth, Waldron, Ssx
Postlip Hall, Winchcombe, Gls
Potterne Manor House, Potterne, Wil
Potterspury Lodge, Potterspury, Nth
Potterton Hall, Barwick in Elmet, Yks
Potto Hall, Whorlton, Yks
Poulton Priory, Poulton, Gls
Pound, Buckland Monachorum, Dev
Poundisford Lodge, Pitminster, Som
Poundon, Poundon, Bkm
Powderham Castle, Powderham, Dev
Pownall Hall, Morley, Chs
Poyle Park, Seale, Sry
Poyntington Manor House, Poyntington, Dor
Poynton Towers, Poynton, Chs
Pradoe, Ruyton of the Eleven Towns, Sal
Preen Manor, Church Preen, Sal
Presbytery (The), Greenwich, Ken
Preshaw House, Exton, Ham
Prestbury House, Prestbury, Gls
Prested Hall, Feering, Ess
Preston Hall, Preston, Rut
Preston House, Preston Candover, Ham
Preston Tower, Eglingham, Nbl
Prestwick Lodge, Dinnington, Nbl
Prestwold Hall, Prestwold, Lei
Prideaux, Luxulyan, Con
Prideaux Place, Padstow, Con
Priestlands, Pennington, Ham
Primley Hill, Paignton, Dev
Prinknash Park, Prinknash Park, Gls
Prior's Court, Powick, Wor
Priory Hill, St Neots, Hun
Priory (The), Ash Priors, Som
Priory (The), Chacombe, Nth
Priory (The), Ipplepen, Dev
Priory (The), Putney, Sry
Priory (The), Seaview, Ham
Priory (The), Usk, Mon
Priory (The), Woodchester, Gls
Puckrup Hall, Twyning, Gls
Puddington Hall, Puddington, Chs
Pudleston Court, Pudleston, Hef
Pull Court, Bushley, Wor
Purley Hall, Purley, Brk
Purley Park, Purley, Brk
Purston Manor, King's Sutton, Nth
Purton House, Purton, Wil
Pusey House, Pusey, Brk
Putley Court, Putley, Hef
Putteridge Bury, Offley, Hrt
Pylewell Park, South Baddesley, Ham
Pynes, Upton Pyne, Dev
Pynkney Hall, Tattersett, Nfk
Pyrford Court, Pyrford, Sry
Pyrgo Park, Havering atte Bower, Ess
Pyrland Hall, Taunton, Som
Pyrton Manor House, Pyrton, Oxf
Pythouse, Tisbury, Wil

Quarry Bank House, Styal, Chs
Quarwood, Nether Swell, Gls
Quatford Castle, Quatford, Sal
Quebec House, East Dereham, Nfk
Quedgeley House, Quedgeley, Gls
Queen Hoo, Tewin, Hrt
Queen's House, Greenwich, Ken
Queens Hill, Ascot, Brk
Queenwood, Chertsey, Sry
Quenby Hall, Quenby, Lei
Quendon Hall, Quendon, Ess
Quernmore Park, Quernmore, Lan
Quex Park, Birchington, Ken
Quidenham Hall, Quidenham, Nfk
Quinta (The), Weston Rhyn, Sal
Quorn House, Quorn, Lei
Quy Hall, Stow-cum-Quy, Cam

Raby Castle, Staindrop, Dur
Rackheath Park, Rackheath, Nfk
Radbourne Hall, Radbourne, Dby
Radway Grange, Radway, War
Ragdale Hall, Ragdale, Lei
Ragley Hall, Arrow, War
Rainscombe House, Oare, Wil
Rainthorpe Hall, Tasburgh, Nfk
Rainworth Lodge, Blidworth, Ntt
Raithby Hall, Raithby near Spilsby, Lin
Ramley, Pennington, Ham
Rampisham Manor, Rampisham, Dor
Rampsbeck, Watermillock, Cul
Ramsbury Manor House, Ramsbury, Wil
Ramsden Hall, Ramsden Crays, Ess
Ramside, Belmont, Dur
Ranby Hall, Babworth, Ntt
Ranby Hall, Ranby, Lin
Ranby House, Babworth, Ntt
Randalls Park, Leatherhead, Sry
Rangemore Hall, Rangemore, Sts
Ranger's House, Greenwich, Ken
Ranksborough, Langham, Rut
Ranston, Iwerne Courtenay, Dor
Ranworth Hall, Ranworth, Nfk
Rapkyns, Slinfold, Ssx
Ratcliffe Hall, Ratcliffe on the Wreake, Lei
Ratclyffe, Clyst Hydon, Dev
Rauceby Hall, South Rauceby, Lin
Raven Cragg, Pooley Bridge, Wes
Ravendale Hall, East Ravendale, Lin
Raveningham Hall, Raveningham, Nfk
Ravenscroft Hall, Ravenscroft, Chs
Ravensden House, Ravensden, Bdf
Ravensthorpe Manor, Felixkirk, Yks
Ravenstone Hall, Ravenstone, Lei
Raynham Hall, East Raynham, Nfk
Read Hall, Read, Lan
Rearsby House, Rearsby, Lei
Red House, Bodicote, Oxf
Red House, Little Blakenham, Sfk
Red House (The), Underskiddaw, Cul

Red Rice House, Upper Clatford, Ham
Red Scar, Grimsargh, Lan
Redbourne Hall, Redbourne, Lin
Rede Hall, Burstow, Sry
Redenham House, Fyfield, Ham
Redfield, Winslow, Bkm
Redfields, Crookham, Ham
Redgrave Hall, Redgrave, Sfk
Redhall, Haughton le Skerne, Dur
Redleaf, Penshurst, Ken
Redlynch House, Redlynch, Wil
Redlynch Park, Redlynch, Som
Redworth Hall, Heighington, Dur
Reedley Hall, Fence, Lan
Reedley Lodge, Fence, Lan
Reedsmouth Hall, Birtley, Nbl
Reeve Castle, Zeal Monachorum, Dev
Reigate Priory, Reigate, Sry
Remnantz, Marlow, Bkm
Rempstone Hall, Corfe Castle, Dor
Rempstone Hall, Rempstone, Ntt
Renishaw Hall, Eckington, Dby
Reston Hall, North Reston, Lin
Retreat (The), Lakenheath, Sfk
Revesby Abbey, Revesby, Lin
Reydon Hall, Reydon, Sfk
Reymerston Hall, Reymerston, Nfk
Rheda, Frizington, Cul
Rhinefield, Brockenhurst, Ham
Rhydd Court, Hanley Castle, Wor
Ribbesford House, Ribbesford, Wor
Ribbleton Hall, Ribbleton, Lan
Ribby Hall, Ribby with Wrea, Lan
Ribston Hall, Great Ribston, Yks
Riccall Hall, Riccall, Yks
Richings Park, Iver, Bkm
Riddings House, Riddings, Dby
Riddlesworth Hall, Riddlesworth, Nfk
Ridge (The), Chapel en le Frith, Dby
Ridge (The), Yate, Gls
Ridley Hall, Beltingham, Nbl
Rigmaden Park, Mansergh, Wes
Rindgale Manor, Fernham, Brk
Ringwould House, Ringwould, Ken
Ripley Castle, Ripley, Yks
Ripon Palace, North Stainley, Yks
Ripple Court, Ripple, Ken
Rippon Hall, Hevingham, Nfk
Ripsley, Milland, Ssx
Riseholme Hall, Riseholme, Lin
Rivenhall Place, Rivenhall, Ess
Riverhill House, Sevenoaks, Ken
Roche Court, Fareham, Ham
Roche Court, Winterslow, Wil
Rochetts, South Weald, Ess
Rochford Lawn, Rochford, Ess
Rockalls Hall, Polstead, Sfk
Rockbeare Court, Rockbeare, Dev
Rockbeare Manor, Rockbeare, Dev
Rockcliffe Park, Darlington, Dur

Rockhurst, West Hoathly, Ssx
Rockingham Castle, Rockingham, Nth
Rockliffe House, Bacup, Lan
Rocks (The), Marshfield, Gls
Rocks (The), Uckfield, Ssx
Roddam Hall, Wooperton, Nbl
Rode Hall, Odd Rode, Chs
Rode Manor, Woolverton, Som
Roehampton House, Putney, Sry
Roeheath House, Chailey, Ssx
Roffey Park, Lower Beeding, Ssx
Rogate Lodge, Rogate, Ssx
Rogerley Hall, Frosterley, Dur
Rogerthorpe Manor, Badsworth, Yks
Roke Manor, Romsey, Ham
Rokeby Park, Rokeby, Yks
Rollesby Hall, Rollesby, Nfk
Rolleston Hall, Rolleston, Lei
Rood Ashton House, West Ashton, Wil
Rookcliff, Milford on Sea, Ham
Rookery Hall, Worleston, Chs
Rookery Park, Yoxford, Sfk
Rookery (The), Dilham, Nfk
Rookery (The), Marlow, Bkm
Rookery (The), Scotby, Cul
Roos Hall, Beccles, Sfk
Ropley Manor, Ropley, Ham
Roscarrack, Budock, Con
Rose Castle, Hawksdale, Cul
Rose Hill, Scotby, Cul
Rosel Manor House, St Martin, Jersey
Ross Court, Ross, Hef
Rossington Hall, Rossington, Yks
Rossway, Northchurch, Hrt
Rostherne Manor House, Rostherne, Chs
Rothamsted, Harpenden, Hrt
Rotherfield Hall, Rotherfield, Ssx
Rotherfield Park, East Tisted, Ham
Rothersyke, Egremont, Cul
Rothley Temple, Rothley, Lei
Rougham Hall, Rougham, Nfk
Rougham Hall, Rougham, Sfk
Roughwood Park, Chalfont St Giles, Bkm
Roundhill Grange, Charlton Musgrove, Som
Roundway Park, Devizes, Wil
Roundwyck, Ebernoe, Ssx
Rounton Grange, East Rounton, Yks
Rous Lench House, Rous Lench, Wor
Rousham House, Rousham, Oxf
Rowdeford House, Bromham, Wil
Rowdell, Washington, Ssx
Rowden Abbey, Bromyard, Hef
Rowfant, Worth, Ssx
Rowfold Grange, Billingshurst, Ssx
Rowlston Hall, Mappleton, Yks
Rownall Hall, Wetley Rocks, Sts
Rowney Priory, Great Munden, Hrt
Rownhams House, Rownhams, Ham
Rowton Castle, Alberbury, Sal
Rowton Hall, Rowton, Chs

Roxholm Hall, Leasingham, Lin
Royal Hill, Tewkesbury, Gls
Royal Lodge, Old Windsor, Brk
Roydon Hall, East Peckham, Ken
Roydon Lodge, Roydon, Ess
Royston Manor, Clayworth, Ntt
Ruckley Grange, Tong, Sal
Rudding Park, Spofforth, Yks
Ruddington Grange, Ruddington, Ntt
Ruddington Hall, Ruddington, Ntt
Rudge Hall, Rudge, Sal
Rufford Abbey, Rufford, Ntt
Rufford Hall, Rufford, Lan
Ruffside Hall, Edmondbyers, Dur
Rumwell Hall, Bishops Hull, Som
Rumwood Court, Langley, Ken
Runwell Hall, Runwell, Ess
Rush Court, Sotwell, Brk
Rushbrooke Hall, Rushbrooke, Sfk
Rushington Manor, Eling, Ham
Rushmore, Berwick St John, Wil
Rushpool Hall, Skelton in Cleveland, Yks
Rushton Hall, Rushton, Nth
Rushwood, Kirklington, Yks
Rusland Hall, Rusland, Lan
Rusper Nunnery, Rusper, Ssx
Russell House, Streatham, Sry
Ruyton Manor, Ruyton of the Eleven Towns, Sal
Ruyton Park, Ruyton of the Eleven Towns, Sal
Rydal Hall, Rydal and Loughrigg, Wes
Ryde House, Ryde, Ham
Rydinghurst, Cranleigh, Sry
Rye Bank House, Edstaston, Sal
Ryelands, Lancaster, Lan
Ryes (The), Little Henny, Ess
Ryngmer Park, Ringmer, Ssx
Ryston Hall, Ryston, Nfk

Sacombe Park, Sacombe, Hrt
Sadborow, Thorncombe, Dor
Saham Hall, Saham Toney, Nfk
Saighton Grange, Saighton, Chs
St Alban's Court, Nonington, Ken
St Anne's Manor, Sutton Bonington, Ntt
St Audries, West Quantoxhead, Som
St Austin's, Boldre, Ham
St Catharine's Court, St Catharine, Som
St Clare, Ryde, Ham
St Clere, Ightham, Ken
St Cleres Hall, St Osyth, Ess
St Edith's, Bromham, Wil
St German's Place, Blackheath, Ken
St Giles's House, Wimborne St Giles, Dor
Saint Hill, East Grinstead, Ssx
St Ives House, Ringwood, Ham
St James' Palace, St James Westminster, Mdx
St James' Priory, Bridgnorth, Sal
St John's Manor, St John, Jersey
St John's, Palgrave, Sfk
St John's Priory, Poling, Ssx

St Johns, Wolsingham, Dur
St Julians, Sevenoaks, Ken
St Leonard's Court, Upton St Leonards, Gls
St Leonard's Forest, Lower Beeding, Ssx
St Leonard's Park, Lower Beeding, Ssx
St Leonards, Clewer Without, Brk
St Leonards House, Nazeing, Ess
St Margaretsbury, Stanstead St Margaret, Hrt
St Mary's Grange, Easthorpe, Ess
St Mary's Hall, Wiggenhall St Mary, Nfk
St Minver House, St Minver, Con
St Osyth's Priory, St Osyth, Ess
St Ouen's Manor, St Ouen, Jersey
St Pauls Walden Bury, St Pauls Walden, Hrt
St Peter's House, St Peter, Jersey
St Pierre Park, St Pierre, Mon
Salhouse Hall, Salhouse, Nfk
Salisbury Palace, Salisbury, Wil
Salkeld Hall, Little Salkeld, Cul
Salle Park, Sall, Nfk
Salperton Park, Salperton, Gls
Salston, Ottery St Mary, Dev
Saltmarshe Castle, Bromyard, Hef
Saltmarshe Hall, Laxton, Yks
Saltram, Plympton St Mary, Dev
Saltwood Castle, Saltwood, Ken
Samares Manor House, St Clement, Jersey
Samlesbury Hall, Samlesbury, Lan
Sanctuary (The), Shobrooke, Dev
Sand Hutton Hall, Sand Hutton near York, Yks
Sandal Grange, Wakefield, Yks
Sandal Hall, Wakefield, Yks
Sandall Grove, Kirk Sandall, Yks
Sandbeck Park, Maltby, Yks
Sandel Manor, Fordingbridge, Ham
Sandford Hall, Claverley, Sal
Sandford Hall, Fauls, Sal
Sandford House, Fulham, Mdx
Sandford Orcas Manor House, Sandford Orcas, Dor
Sandford Orleigh, Highweek, Dev
Sandford Park, Sandford St Martin, Oxf
Sandford, Wareham, Dor
Sandhall, Howden, Yks
Sandhills, Christchurch, Ham
Sandhurst Lodge, Sandhurst, Brk
Sandiway House, Weaverham, Chs
Sandleford Priory, Sandleford, Brk
Sandling Park, Saltwood, Ken
Sandling Place, Boxley, Ken
Sandon Hall, Sandon, Sts
Sandridge Park, Stoke Gabriel, Dev
Sandringham House, Sandringham, Nfk
Sands Hall, Sedgefield, Dur
Sandybrook Hall, Offcote, Dby
Sandywell Park, Dowdeswell, Gls
Sanham House, Kirby Bellars, Lei
Sansaw, Clive, Sal
Sarnesfield Court, Sarnesfield, Hef
Saumarez House, Castel, Guernsey
Sausmarez Manor, St Martin, Guernsey

Sausthorpe Hall, Sausthorpe, Lin
Savernake Forest, Savernake Forest, Wil
Sawley Hall, Sawley near Ripon, Yks
Sawston Hall, Sawston, Cam
Saxby Hall, Saxby All Saints, Lin
Saxelbye Park, Grimston, Lei
Saxham Hall, Great Saxham, Sfk
Saxlingham Hall, Saxlingham Nethergate, Nfk
Saxlingham Lodge, Saxlingham Nethergate, Nfk
Scadbury Park, Chislehurst, Ken
Scalby Hall, Scalby, Yks
Scaleby Castle, Scaleby, Cul
Scaleby Hall, Scaleby, Cul
Scalesceugh, Carleton, Cul
Scampston Hall, Rillington, Yks
Scampton House, Scampton, Lin
Scanlands, Sway, Ham
Scar House, Arkengarthdale, Yks
Scargill Lodge, Barningham, Yks
Scarisbrick Hall, Scarisbrick, Lan
Scarthingwell Hall, Saxon, Yks
Scarthwaite, Quernmore, Lan
Scawby Grove, Scawby, Lin
Scawby Hall, Scawby, Lin
Scorrier House, Gwennap, Con
Scotney Castle, Lamberhurst, Ken
Scottow Hall, Scottow, Nfk
Scrafton Lodge, Coverham, Yks
Scraptoft Hall, Scraptoft, Lei
Scratby Hall, Ormesby St Margaret, Nfk
Scrivelsby Court, Scrivelsby, Lin
Scriven Park, Scriven, Yks
Scruton Hall, Scruton, Yks
Sea Grove, Seaview, Ham
Seaborough Court, Seaborough, Dor
Seacox Heath, Flimwell, Ssx
Searles, Fletching, Ssx
Seat How, Thornthwaite, Cul
Seaton Delaval Hall, Blyth, Nbl
Seaview House, Seaview, Ham
Seckford Hall, Great Bealings, Sfk
Sedbury Park, Gilling West near Richmond, Yks
Sedgebrook Manor, Sedgebrook, Lin
Sedgeford Hall, Sedgeford, Nfk
Sedgwick House, Sedgwick, Wes
Sedgwick Park, Nuthurst, Ssx
Seend Lodge, Seend, Wil
Seething Old Hall, Seething, Nfk
Sefton Park, Stoke Poges, Bkm
Seighford Hall, Seighford, Sts
Seigneurie (The), Sark, Sark
Selaby Hall, Darlingon, Dur
Sellarsbrook Court, Ganarew, Hef
Sendholme, Send, Sry
Sennicots, Funtington, Ssx
Sennowe Hall, Stibbard, Nfk
Serlby Hall, Harworth, Ntt
Settrington House, Settrington, Yks
Seven Springs, Cubberley, Gls
Severn Bank, Severn Stoke, Wor

Severn End, Hanley Castle, Wor
Seymour Court, Marlow, Bkm
Sezincote House, Sezincote, Gls
Shadingfield Hall, Shadingfield, Sfk
Shadwell Court, Shadwell, Nfk
Shakenhurst, Bayton, Wor
Shalden Manor, Shalden, Ham
Shalford Hall, Shelford, Cam
Shallcross Manor, Fernilee, Dby
Shalstone Manor, Shalstone, Bkm
Shanks House, Cucklington, Som
Shapwick House, Shapwick, Som
Shardeloes, Amersham, Bkm
Sharnden, Mayfield, Ssx
Sharow Hall, Sharow, Yks
Sharpham, Ashrington, Dev
Sharrow Bay, Pooley Bridge, Wes
Sharsted Court, Doddington, Ken
Shavington Hall, Moreton Say, Sal
Shaw Hill, Shaw, Wil
Shaw Hill, Whittle le Woods, Lan
Shaw House, Shaw, Brk
Shawdon Hall, Whittingham, Nbl
Shawford House, Twyford, Ham
Shedfield House, Shedfield, Ham
Sheen Cottage, Richmond, Sry
Sheffield Park, Fletching, Ssx
Shelbrook Hill, Dudleston, Sal
Shelley Hall, Shelley, Ess
Shelsley Court House, Shelsley Walsh, Wor
Shelswell Park, Shelswell, Oxf
Shenley Hill, Shenley, Hrt
Shenley Park, Shenley Church End, Bkm
Shenton Hall, Shenton, Lei
Shephall Bury, Shephall, Hrt
Sherborne Castle, Castleton, Dor
Sherborne Park, Sherborne, Gls
Sherbourne House, Sherbourne, War
Shere Manor House, Shere, Sry
Sheriff Hutton Park, Sheriff Hutton, Yks
Sheringham Hall, Upper Sheringham, Nfk
Shermanbury Grange, Shermanbury, Ssx
Shernfold Park, Frant, Ssx
Sherridge, Leigh Sinton, Wor
Sherwood Lodge, Arnold, Ntt
Shillinglee Park, Kirdford, Ssx
Shillingstone Grange, Shillingstone, Dor
Shillingthorpe Hall, Braceborough and Wilsthorpe, Lin
Shipley Hall, Shipley, Dby
Shipton Court, Shipton under Wychwood, Oxf
Shipton Manor, Shipton Bellinger, Ham
Shirburn Castle, Shirburn, Oxf
Shire Newton Hall, Shirenewton, Mon
Shirley Hall, Langton, Ken
Shirrenden, Horsmonden, Ken
Shobdon Court, Shobdon, Hef
Shobrooke Park, Shobrooke, Dev
Shockerwick House, Bathford, Som
Sholebroke Lodge, Whittlebury, Nth
Shoreham Place, Shoreham, Ken

Shoreston Hall, Sea Houses, Nbl
Shortgrove Hall, Newport, Ess
Shortridge Hall, Warkworth, Nbl
Shotesham Park, Shotesham, Nfk
Shotley Hall, Shotley, Nbl
Shotley Park, Shotley Bridge, Dur
Shotover House, Forest Hill, Oxf
Shottesbrooke Park, Shottesbrooke, Brk
Shotton Hall, Hadnall, Sal
Shotwick Park, Great Saughall, Chs
Shrigley Hall, Pott Shrigley, Chs
Shropham Hall, Shropham, Nfk
Shrubbery (The), Ilminster, Som
Shrubland Park, Barham, Sfk
Shuckburgh Park, Upper Shuckburgh, War
Shudy Camps Park, Shudy Camps, Cam
Shugborough Hall, Great Haywood, Sts
Sibdon Castle, Sibdon Carwood, Sal
Sibton Abbey, Sibton, Sfk
Sibton Park, Lyminge, Ken
Sidbury Manor, Sidbury, Dev
Siddington Hall, Siddington, Gls
Sidestrand Hall, Sidestrand, Nfk
Sigglesthorne Hall, Sigglesthorne, Yks
Silksworth Hall, Silksworth, Dur
Silksworth House, Silksworth, Dur
Silvermere, Walton on Thames, Sry
Silwood Park, Sunninghill, Brk
Singleton Park, Kendal, Wes
Singleton Park, Singleton, Lan
Sinton Court, Grimley, Wor
Sion Hill House, Wolverley, Wor
Sion Hill, Kirby Wiske, Yks
Sissinghurst Castle, Sissinghurs, Ken
Sissinghurst Court, Sissinghurst, Ken
Sissinghurst Place, Sissinghurst, Ken
Sizergh Place, Helsington, Wes
Skeffington Hall, Skeffington, Lei
Skegby Hall, Skegby, Ntt
Skelbrook Hall, Skelbrook, Yks
Skelton Castle, Skelton in Cleveland, Yks
Skelton Hall, Skelton, Yks
Skelton Manor House, Skelton, Yks
Skendleby Hall, Skendleby, Lin
Skilts, Studley, War
Skipton Castle, Skipton, Yks
Skipwith Hall, Skipwith, Yks
Skirsgill Park, Penrith, Cul
Skirwith Abbey, Skirwith, Cul
Skutterskelfe Hall, Rudby in Cleveland, Yks
Slade, Cornwood, Dev
Slade House (The), Podington, Bdf
Slape Manor, Netherbury, Dor
Slaugham Park, Slaugham, Ssx
Slaugham Place, Slaugham, Ssx
Sledmere House, Sledmere, Yks
Sleningford Park, North Stainley, Yks
Slindon House, Slindon, Ssx
Slinfold Lodge, Slinfold, Ssx
Sloe House, Halstead, Ess

Sloley Hall, Sloley, Nfk
Slyfield Manor, Great Bookham, Sry
Small Downs House, Worth, Ken
Smallburgh Hall, Smallburgh, Nfk
Smalley Hall, Smalley, Dby
Smedmore, Kimmeridge, Dor
Smeetham Hall, Bulmer, Ess
Snakemoor, Durley, Ham
Snape Hill, Rickinghill Inferior, Sfk
Snape, Tidebrook, Ssx
Snarehill Hall, Snarehill, Nfk
Sneaton Hall, Sneaton, Yks
Snelston Hall, Snelston, Dby
Snettisham Old Hall, Snettisham, Nfk
Sniperley Hall, Witton Gilbert, Dur
Snittlegarth, Bewaldeth, Cul
Snowdenham Hall, Bramley, Sry
Snowfield, Bearsted, Ken
Snydale Hall, Normanton, Yks
Sockburn Hall, Sockburn, Dur
Sodylt, Dudleston, Sal
Solberge, Kirby Wiske, Yks
Somborne Park, King's Somborne, Ham
Somerby Hall, Corringham, Lin
Somerby Hall, Somerby, Lei
Somerby Hall, Somerby (North Lincs), Lin
Somerhill Park, Tonbridge, Ken
Somerley, Harbridge, Ham
Somerleyton Hall, Somerleyton, Sfk
Somersal Herbert Hall, Somersal Herbert, Dby
Somerset Court, Brent Knoll, Som
Somerset House, Strand, Mdx
Somerton Court, Somerton, Som
Somerton Erleigh, Somerton, Som
Somerton Hall, West Somerton, Nfk
Sompting Abbotts, Sompting, Ssx
Sopley Park, Sopley, Ham
Sortridge, Sandford, Dev
Sotterley Hall, Sotterley, Sfk
South Allington House, Chivelstone, Dev
South Hartfield House, Coleman's Hatch, Ssx
South Hill Park, Easthampstead, Brk
South Leigh Park, Warblington, Ham
South Lodge, Lower Beeding, Ssx
South Luffenham Hall, South Luffenham, Rut
South Lytchett Manor House, Lytchett Minster, Dor
South Park, Penshurst, Ken
South Walsham Hall, South Walsham, Nfk
South Wraxall Manor, South Wraxall, Wil
Southam de la Bere, Bishop's Cleeve, Gls
Southgate House, Clown, Dby
Southill Park, Southill, Bdf
Southington House, Overton, Ham
Southover House, Tolpuddle, Dor
Southwick Hall, Southwick, Nth
Southwick Park, Southwick, Ham
Southwood House, Tiverton, Dev
Southwood, Leigh, Ken
Spains Hall, Finchingfield, Ess
Sparkford Hall, Sparkford, Som

Sparsholt Manor House, Sparsholt, Brk
Sparth House, Clayton le Moors, Lan
Spaynes Hall, Great Yeldham, Ess
Speke Hall, Speke, Lan
Spellow Hill, Staveley, Yks
Spencer Hall, Great Yeldham, Ess
Spencer House, Blackheath, Ken
Spetchley Park, Spetchley, Wor
Spexhall Manor House, Spexhall, Sfk
Spillsill Court, Staplehurst, Ken
Spinfield, Marlow, Bkm
Spitchwick Manor, Leusdon, Dev
Spixworth Park, Spixworth, Nfk
Spondon Hall, Spondon, Dby
Spratton Grange, Spratton, Nth
Spratton Hall, Spratton, Nth
Spring Grove, Wribbenhall, Wor
Spring Grove, Wye, Ken
Springfield, Egremont, Cul
Springfield, Hackney, Mdx
Springfield Hall, Lancaster, Lan
Springfield House, Knowle, War
Springfield Park, Hackney, Mdx
Sproughton Manor House, Sproughton, Sfk
Sprowston Hall, Sprowston, Nfk
Sprowston Lodge, Sprowston, Nfk
Sprydoncote, Broadclyst, Dev
Spye Park, Chittoe, Wil
Squerryes Court, Westerham, Ken
Stackley House, Great Glen, Lei
Staffield Hall, Staffield, Cul
Stafford House, West Stafford, Dor
Stagenhoe Park, St Pauls Walden, Hrt
Stagshaw House, St John Lee, Nbl
Staindrop House, Staindrop, Dur
Stainsby House, Smalley, Dby
Stakes Hill Lodge, Waterlooville, Ham
Stanage Park, Brampton Bryan, Hef
Stanbridge Earls, Romsey, Ham
Stanbridge Grange, Staplefield, Ssx
Stanbury, Grazeley, Brk
Standen, East Grinstead, Ssx
Standen House, Chute, Wil
Standen House, South Arreton, Ham
Standerwick Court, Beckington, Som
Standish Hall, Standish, Lan
Stanfield Hall, Wymondham, Nfk
Stanfield House, Hampstead, Mdx
Stanford Court, Stanford on Teme, Wor
Stanford Hall, Stanford, Nth
Stanford Park, Stanford on Soar, Ntt
Stanford Park, Westrill, Lei
Stanford Place, Stanford in the Vale, Brk
Stanhill Court, Charlwood, Sry
Stanhoe Hall, Stanhoe, Nfk
Stanhope Castle, Stanhope, Dur
Stanlake Park, Hurst, Brk
Stanley Grange, Stanley, Yks
Stanley Hall, Astley Abbotts, Sal
Stanley House, Kings Stanley, Gls

Stanley Park, Selsley, Gls
Stanmer, Stanmer, Ssx
Stanmore Hall, Worfield, Sal
Stanshawes Court, Yate, Gls
Stanstead Bury, Stanstead Abbotts, Hrt
Stanstead Hall, Felstead, Ess
Stansted Hall, Stansted, Ess
Stansted House, Stansted, Ess
Stansted Park, Stansted, Ssx
Stanthorne Hall, Stanthorne, Chs
Stanton Court, Stanton, Gls
Stanton Hall, Stanton in the Peak, Dby
Stanton House, Stanton Fitzwarren, Wil
Stanton Woodhouse, Stanton in the Peak, Dby
Stanway House, Stanway, Gls
Stanwell Place, Stanwell, Mdx
Stanwick House, Stanwick, Nth
Staplefield Place, Staplefield, Ssx
Stapleford Park, Stapleford, Lei
Staplegrove Manor, Staplegrove, Som
Staplehurst Place, Staplehurst, Ken
Stargroves, East Woodhay, Ham
Starston Place, Starston, Nfk
Startford Hills, Stratford St Mary, Sfk
Statfold Hall, Thorpe Constantine, Sts
Statham Lodge, Lymm, Chs
Staughton Manor, Great Staughton, Hun
Staunton Hall, Staunton, Ntt
Staunton Harold, Staunton Harold, Lei
Staverton Court, Staverton, Gls
Staverton House, Staverton, Gls
Steane Park, Steane, Nth
Stedcombe Manor, Axmouth, Dev
Stedham Hall, Stedham, Ssx
Steephill Castle, Ventnor, Ham
Steepleton House, Steepleton Iwerne, Dor
Steepleton Manor, Winterbourne Steepleton, Dor
Stella Hall, Stella, Dur
Stenigot House, Stenigot, Lin
Stentwood House, Dunkeswell Abbey, Dev
Stetchworth Park, Stetchworth, Cam
Steventon Manor, Steventon, Ham
Stinsford House, Stinsford, Dor
Stirtloe House, Buckden, Hun
Stisted Hall, Stisted, Ess
Stobars Hall, Kirkby Stephen, Wes
Stoberry Park, Wells, Som
Stock Hill, Gillingham, Dor
Stock House, Stock Gaylard, Dor
Stock Park, Finsthwaite, Lan
Stockeld Park, Spofforth, Yks
Stocken Hall, Stretton, Rut
Stockgrove, Soulbury, Bkm
Stockland Bristol Manor House, Stockland Bristol, Som
Stockton Hall, Stockton in the Forest, Yks
Stockton House, Stockton, Wil
Stockwell Hall, Little Burstead, Ess
Stockwood, Luton, Bdf
Stodham Park, Liss, Ham
Stoke Albany House, Stoke Albany, Nth

INDEX OF ENGLISH COUNTRY HOUSES

Stoke College, Stoke by Clare, Sfk
Stoke Dabernon Manor House, Stoke Dabernon, Sry
Stoke Edith Park, Stoke Edith, Hef
Stoke Golding Lodge, Stoke Golding, Lei
Stoke, Greet, Sal
Stoke Hall, Acton, Chs
Stoke Hall, East Stoke, Ntt
Stoke Hall, Stoke, Dby
Stoke Hall, Stoke Holy Cross, Nfk
Stoke Lodge, Stoke St Milborough, Sal
Stoke Park, Stoke Bruerne, Nth
Stoke Place, Stoke Poges, Bkm
Stoke Priory, Stoke by Nayland, Sfk
Stoke Rochford, Stoke Rochford, Lin
Stokesay Court, Stokesay, Sal
Stokesley, Stokenham, Dev
Stoketon, St Stephen by Saltash, Con
Ston Easton Park, Ston Easton, Som
Stone Castle, Stone near Dartford, Ken
Stone House, Stone, Wor
Stoneham Park, North Stoneham, Ham
Stonehouse Court, Stonehouse, Gls
Stoneleigh Abbey, Stoneleigh, War
Stonerwood Park, Steep, Ham
Stonewall Park, Chiddingstone, Ken
Stoney Middleton Hall, Stoney Middleton, Dby
Stoney Thorpe, Long Itchington, War
Stoney Ware, Bisham, Brk
Stonor Park, Pishill, Oxf
Stopham House, Stopham, Ssx
Stott Park House, Finsthwaite, Lan
Stourhead, Stourton, Wil
Stourton Castle, Kinver, Sts
Stourton Hall, Baumber, Lin
Stow Hall, Stow Bardolph, Nfk
Stowell Park, Stowell, Gls
Stowell Park, Wilcot, Wil
Stowlangtoft Hall, Stowlangtoft, Sfk
Stradishall Place, Stradishall, Sfk
Stradsett Hall, Stradsett, Nfk
Stragglethorpe Old Hall, Stragglethorpe, Lin
Strangways, Marnhull, Dor
Stratfield Saye House, Stratfield Saye, Ham
Stratton Audley Hall, Stratton Audley, Oxf
Stratton Chase, Chalfont St Giles, Bkm
Stratton House, Stratton, Gls
Stratton Manor House, Long Stratton, Nfk
Stratton Park, Stratton St Margaret, Wil
Stratton Strawless Hall, Stratton Strawless, Nfk
Strattonend, Stratton, Gls
Streatley House, Streatley, Brk
Street Court, Kingsland, Hef
Strelley Hall, Strelley, Ntt
Strensham Court, Strensham, Wor
Strete Ralegh, Whimple, Dev
Stretton Hall, Stretton en le Field, Lei
Stretton Hall, Stretton near Brewood, Sts
Strickstenning Hall, Much Birch, Hef
Strode, Ermington, Dev
Strode Manor, Netherbury, Dor

Strode Park, Herne, Ken
Strood Park, Slinfold, Ssx
Strumpshaw Hall, Strumpshaw, Nfk
Stubbers, North Ockendon, Ess
Stubton Hall, Stubton, Lin
Stuckeridge, Oakford, Dev
Studley Priory, Horton cum Studley, Oxf
Studley Royal, Studley Royal, Yks
Study (The), Bonsall, Dby
Stukeley Hall, Great Stukeley, Hun
Stutton Hall, Stutton, Sfk
Styche Hall, Moreton Say, Sal
Styford Hall, Bywell, Nbl
Sudbourne Hall, Sudbourne, Sfk
Sudbury Hall, Sudbury, Dby
Sudeley Castle, Sudeley Manor, Gls
Sudgrove House, Miserden, Gls
Sufton, Mordiford, Hef
Sugnall House, Eccleshall, Sts
Sugwas Court, Stretton Sugwas, Hef
Sulby Hall, Sulby, Nth
Sulham House, Sulham, Brk
Sulhamstead House, Sulhamstead, Brk
Summer Hill, Egton cum Newland, Lan
Summerlands, Heversham, Wes
Summers Place, Blllingshurst, Ssx
Sunderlandwick Hall, Hutton Cranswick, Yks
Sundorne Castle, Uffington, Sal
Sunningdale Park, Sunningdale, Brk
Sunninghill Park, Sunninghill, Brk
Sutherland Lodge, Cropton, Yks
Sutton Court, Stowey, Som
Sutton Hall, Barcombe, Ssx
Sutton Hall, Sutton Bonington, Ntt
Sutton Hall, Sutton on the Forest, Yks
Sutton Hoo, Bromeswell, Sfk
Sutton Park, Sutton, Bdf
Sutton Place, Woking, Sry
Sutton Rock, Sutton cum Duckmanton, Dby
Suttons, Stapleford Tawney, Ess
Swaffham Prior House, Swaffham Prior, Cam
Swaines House, Bembridge, Ham
Swainston, Calbourne, Ham
Swalcliffe Park, Swalcliffe, Oxf
Swallowfield, Nuthurst, Ssx
Swallowfield Park, Swallowfield, Brk
Swanmore House, Swanmore, Ham
Swannington Court, Swannington, Nfk
Swannington House, Swannington, Lei
Swanton Hall, Swanton Abbot, Nfk
Swarcliffe Birstwith, Swarcliffe Birstwith, Yks
Sweeney Hall, Oswestry, Sal
Swerford Park, Swerford, Oxf
Swettenham Hall, Swettenham, Chs
Swift's House, Stoke Lyne, Oxf
Swifts Place, Cranbrook, Ken
Swinburne Castle, Chollerton, Nbl
Swindon Manor, Swindon, Gls
Swinfen Hall, Weeford, Sts
Swinhope House, Swinhope, Lin

Swinithwaite Hall, West Witton, Yks
Swinstead Hall, Swinstead, Lin
Swinton Grange, Appleton le Street, Yks
Swinton Park, Masham, Yks
Swithland Hall, Swithland, Lei
Swyncombe House, Swyncombe, Oxf
Swynnerton Park, Swynnerton, Sts
Swythamley Park, Rushton Spencer, Sts
Syde House, Syde, Gls
Sydenham House, Marystowe, Dev
Sydling Court, Sydling St Nicholas, Dor
Sydmonton Court, Sydmonton, Ham
Sydnope Hall, Darley Dale, Dby
Syerston Hall, Syerston, Ntt
Syndale House, Ospringe, Ken
Syon House, Isleworth, Mdx
Syston Court, Syston, Gls
Syston Park, Syston, Lin
Sywell Hall, Sywell, Nth

Tabley House, Nether Tabley, Chs
Tackley Park, Tackley, Oxf
Tacolneston Hall, Tacolneston, Nfk
Tainfield House, Kingston near Taunton, Som
Tallantire Hall, Tallantire, Cul
Talycoed Court, Llanvihangel-Ystern-Llewern, Mon
Tandridge Court, Tandridge, Sry
Tanfield Lodge, West Tanfield, Yks
Tangier Park, Wootton St Lawrence, Ham
Tanners Manor, Waldron, Ssx
Tapley Park, Westleigh, Dev
Taplow Court, Taplow, Bkm
Tarn House, Skipton, Yks
Tarn Lodge, Castle Carrock, Cul
Tarrant Gunville Manor House, Tarrant Gunville, Dor
Tasburgh Hall, Tasburgh, Nfk
Tatchbury Manor House, Netley Marsh, Ham
Tathwell Hall, Tathwell, Lin
Tattingstone Place, Tattingstone, Sfk
Tatton Park, Tatton, Chs
Taverham Hall, Taverham, Nfk
Tawsden, Brenchley, Ken
Tawstock Court, Tawstock, Dev
Taynton House, Taynton, Gls
Teddesley Hall, Teddesley Hay, Sts
Tedsmore Hall, West Felton, Sal
Tedstone Court, Tedstone Delamere, Hef
Teeton Manor House, Ravensthorpe, Nth
Teffont Manor, Teffont Ewyas, Wil
Temple Combe, Wargrave, Brk
Temple Grafton Court, Temple Grafton, War
Templeton, Putney, Sry
Tendring Hall, Stoke by Nayland, Sfk
Terling Place, Terling, Ess
Terlings Park, Gilston, Hrt
Terry Bank, Mansergh, Wes
Tettenhall Towers, Tettenhall, Sts
Tetton House, Kingston near Taunton, Som
Tetworth Hall, Gamlingay, Cam
Tetworth Hall, Tetworth, Hun

Tew Park, Great Tew, Oxf
Tewin Water, Tewin, Hrt
Tewkesbury Park, Tewkesbury, Gls
Thame Park, Thame, Oxf
Thatcham House, Thatcham, Brk
Thatched House Lodge, Richmond, Sry
Theakston Hall, Burneston, Yks
Theberton Hall, Therberton, Sfk
Theberton House, Theberton, Sfk
Thedden Grange, Alton, Ham
Thelveton Hall, Thelveton, Nfk
Thelwall Hall, Thelwall, Chs
Thenford House, Thenford, Nth
Thicket Priory, Thorganby, Yks
Thickthorn Hall, Hethersett, Nfk
Thimbleby Hall, Osmotherley, Yks
Thirlestaine House, Cheltenham, Gls
Thirsk Hall, Thirsk, Yks
Thistlewood, Stockdalewrath, Cul
Thoby Priory, Mountnessing, Ess
Thonock Hall, Thonock, Lin
Thoresby Park, Perlethorpe, Ntt
Thorganby Hall, Thorganby, Lin
Thorington Hall, Thorington, Sfk
Thorn, Wembury, Dev
Thornbridge Hall, Ashford, Dby
Thornbury Castle, Thornbury, Gls
Thornbury Park, Thornbury, Gls
Thornby Hall, Thornby, Nth
Thornby House, Thornby, Nth
Thorncombe, Bramley, Sry
Thorne Court, Shimpling, Sfk
Thorne House, Thorne Coffin, Som
Thorney Island Manor House, Thorney Island, Ssx
Thorngrove, Grimley, Wor
Thornham Hall, Thornham Magna, Sfk
Thornham Hall, Thornham, Nfk
Thornham Manor House, Thornham, Nfk
Thornhaugh Hall, Thornhaugh, Nth
Thornhill, Stalbridge, Dor
Thornton Hall, Thornton Dale, Yks
Thornton Watlass Hall, Thornton Watlass, Yks
Thornycroft Hall, Siddington, Chs
Thorp Perrow, Well, Yks
Thorpe Abbotts Place, Thorpe Abbotts, Nfk
Thorpe Hall, Peterborough, Nth
Thorpe Hall, Rudston, Yks
Thorpe Hall, South Elkington, Lin
Thorpe Hall, Thorpe Constantine, Sts
Thorpe Hall, Thorpe le Soken, Ess
Thorpe Hall, Thorpe St Andrew, Nfk
Thorpe High House, Thorpe St Andrew, Nfk
Thorpe House, Thorpe, Sry
Thorpe Lubenham Hall, Thorpe Lubenham, Nth
Thorpe Malsor Hall, Thorpe Malsor, Nth
Thorpe Satchville Hall, Thorpe Satchville, Lei
Thorpland Hall, Fakenham, Nfk
Threekingham House, Threekingham, Lin
Throope Manor, Bishopstone near Salisbury, Wil
Thrumpton Hall, Thrumpton, Ntt

INDEX OF ENGLISH COUNTRY HOUSES

Thruxton Manor House, Thruxton, Ham
Thurgarton House, Thurgarton, Nfk
Thurland Castle, Tunstall, Lan
Thurlby Hall, Thurlby near Lincoln, Lin
Thurnham Court, Thurnham, Ken
Thurnham Hall, Thurnham, Lan
Thurning Hall, Thurning, Nfk
Thurston End Hall, Hawkedon, Sfk
Thurston House, Thurston, Sfk
Thurstonville, Egton cum Newland, Lan
Tibberton Court, Tibberton, Gls
Tichborne Park, Tichborne, Ham
Tickencote Hall, Tickencote, Rut
Tickhill Castle, Tickhill, Yks
Tickwood Hall, Much Wenlock, Sal
Tiddington House, Albury, Oxf
Tidenham House, Tidenham, Gls
Tidmarsh Grange, Tidmarsh, Brk
Tidmarsh Manor, Tidmarsh, Brk
Tile House, Lillingstone Dayrell, Bkm
Tilgate, Worth, Ssx
Tillingbourne, Wotton, Sry
Tillmouth Park, Cornhill, Nbl
Tilstone Lodge, Tilstone Fearnall, Chs
Timewell House, Morebath, Dev
Timsbury House, Timsbury, Som
Tingrith Manor, Tingrith, Bdf
Tirley Garth, Willington, Chs
Tissington Hall, Tissington, Dby
Titlington Hall, Eglingham, Nbl
Titsey Place, Titsey, Sry
Tittensor Chase, Tittensor, Sts
Tiverton Castle, Tiverton, Dev
Tixover Grange, Tixover, Rut
Tixover Hall, Tixover, Rut
Tockington Manor, Olveston, Gls
Toddington Manor, Toddington, Bdf
Toddington Manor, Toddington, Gls
Todenham House, Todenham, Gls
Toft Hall, Toft, Chs
Tolethorpe Hall, Little Casterton, Rut
Tollesby Hall, Marton, Yks
Tolson Hall, Strickland Ketel, Wes
Tonacombe Manor House, Morwenstow, Con
Tongswood, Hawkhurst, Ken
Tor Newton House, Torbryan, Dev
Tor Side, Haslingden, Lan
Torry Hill, Lenham, Ken
Tortworth Court, Tortworth, Gls
Tostock Place, Tostock, Sfk
Tothby Manor, Alford, Lin
Totley Hall, Totley, Dby
Totteridge Park, Totteridge, Hrt
Totterton Hall, Lydbury North, Sal
Tottingworth Park, Heathfield, Ssx
Tower Court, South Ascot, Brk
Tower House, Woodchester, Gls
Towers (The), Cockermouth, Cul
Townhead, Staveley, Lan
Tracey, Awliscombe, Dev

Tracy Park, Downton, Gls
Trafalgar, Standlynch, Wil
Treago Castle, St Weonards, Hef
Trebartha Hall, North Hill, Con
Trebursye, South Petherwin, Con
Tredegar Park, Bassaleg, Mon
Tredethy, St Mabyn, Con
Tredilion Park, Llantilio-Pertholey, Mon
Trefusis, Flushing, Con
Tregaddick, Blisland, Con
Tregeare, Laneast, Con
Tregonthnan, St Michael Penkevil, Con
Tregrehan, St Blazey, Con
Tregye, Devoran, Con
Trehane, Probus, Con
Trehill, Kenn, Dev
Trelaske, Lewannick, Con
Trelawne, Pelynt, Con
Trelissick, Feock, Con
Trelowarren, Mawgan in Meneage, Con
Trematon Castle, St Stephen by Saltash, Con
Trematon Hall, St Stephen by Saltash, Con
Tremeer, St Tudy, Con
Trenant Park, Duloe, Con
Trengwainton, Hea Moor, Con
Trent Park, Enfield, Mdx
Trereife, Madron, Con
Tresco Abbey, Tresco, Con
Tresilian House, St Newlyn East, Con
Trethill House, Sheviock, Con
Trevarno, Sithney, Con
Trevayler, Gulval, Con
Treverven House, St Buryan, Con
Trevethoe, Lelant, Con
Trevince, Gwennap, Con
Trevissome, Mylor, Con
Trewan, St Columb Major, Con
Trewardale, Blisland, Con
Trewarthenick, Cornelly, Con
Trewern Hall, Hengoed cum Gobowen, Sal
Trewhitt Hall, Rothbury, Nbl
Trewidden, Madron, Con
Trewince, Gerrans, Con
Trewithen, Probus, Con
Treworgey House, Liskeard, Con
Trewornan, St Minver, Con
Trewsbury, Coates, Gls
Trewyn, Cwmyoy, Mon
Triley Court, Llantilio-Pertholey, Mon
Tring Park, Tring, Hrt
Trinity Manor House, Trinity, Jersey
Triscombe House, West Bagborough, Som
Tristford, Harberton, Dev
Trood House, Exminster, Dev
Trosley Towers, Stansted, Ken
Troston Hall, Troston, Sfk
Trulls Hatch, Mayfield, Ssx
Trumpington Hall, Trumpington, Cam
Trusley Manor, Trusley, Dby
Tubney House, Tubney, Brk

43

Tuddenham Hall, Tuddenham St Martin, Sfk
Tuddenham Lodge, Tuddenham, Nfk
Tunstall Hall, Norton in Hales, Sal
Turkdean Manor, Turkdean, Gls
Turnworth House, Turnworth, Dor
Turvey Abbey, Turvey, Bdf
Turvey House, Turvey, Bdf
Turville Park, Turville, Bkm
Turweston House, Turweston, Bkm
Tushingham Hall, Tushingham, Chs
Tusmore House, Tusmore, Oxf
Twemlow Hall, Twemlow, Chs
Twineham Grange, Twineham, Ssx
Twizell House, Lucker, Nbl
Twyford Hall, Twyford, Nfk
Twyn Bell, Llanbadoc, Mon
Twyning Manor, Twyning, Gls
Twyning Park, Twyning, Gls
Tyberton Court, Tyberton, Hef
Tylney Hall, Rotherwick, Ham
Tyn-y-Rhos Hall, Weston Rhyn, Sal
Tyneham House, Tyneham, Dor
Tyntesfield, West Bagborough, Som
Tyringham House, Tyringham, Bkm
Tyrrels, Shepworth, Cam
Tytherington Grange, Tytherington, Gls
Tythrop House, Tythrop, Oxf
Tyttenhanger Park, London Colney and Ridge, Hrt

Uckfield House, Uckfield, Ssx
Uddens House, Holt, Dor
Uffington House, Uffington, Lin
Ufford Hall, Ufford, Nth
Ufford Place, Ufford, Sfk
Ufton Court, Ufton, Brk
Ugbrooke, Chudleigh, Dev
Ulceby Manor, Ulceby with Fordington, Lin
Ullenwood House, Cubberley, Gls
Ullesthorpe Court, Claybrooke, Lei
Ulverscroft Cottage, Ulverscroft, Lei
Umberslade, Tanworth in Arden, War
Underley Hall, Kirkby Lonsdale, Wes
Unsted Park, Bramley, Sry
Unthank Hall, Haltwhistle, Nbl
Up Cerne Manor, Up Cerne, Dor
Up Ottery Manor, Up Ottery, Dev
Up Park, Harting, Ssx
Upcott Avenel, Sheepwash, Dev
Upcott, Pilton, Dev
Uphill Manor, Uphill, Som
Upland Hall, Bungay, Sfk
Upper Gatton Park, Gatton, Sry
Upper Grove House, Putney, Sry
Upper Helmsley Hall, Upper Helmsley, Yks
Upton Grey House, Upton Grey, Ham
Upton Grove, Tetbury Upton, Gls
Upton Hall, Upton near Northampton, Nth
Upton Hall, Upton, Ntt
Upton House, Broadstone, Dor
Upton House, Old Alresford, Ham

Upton House, Ratley, War
Upton House, Tetbury Upton, Gls
Upton House, Worth, Ken
Upwood House, Upwood, Hun
Upwood Park, Marcham, Brk
Urchfont Manor, Urchfont, Wil
Utterby House, Utterby, Lin
Utterby Manor, Utterby, Lin

Vache (The), Chalfont St Giles, Bkm
Vale Royal, Whitegate, Chs
Valence, Westerham, Ken
Vanbrugh Castle, Greenwich, Ken
Vane House, Hampstead, Mdx
Vasterne Manor, Wootton Bassett, Wil
Ven, Milborne Port, Som
Venn, Lamerton, Dev
Vennwood, Bodenham, Hef
Verdley, Fernhurst, Ssx
Vereley, Burley, Ham
Vicar's Cross, Great Boughton, Chs
Vicar's Hill, Boldre, Ham
Vinchelez de Bas Manor, St Ouen, Jersey
Vinchelez de Haut Manor, St Ouen, Jersey
Vine House, Hampstead, Mdx
Vinehall, Mountfield, Ssx
Vinters, Boxley, Ken
Volta House, Hampstead, Mdx
Vyne (The), Sherborne St John, Ham

Waddesdon Manor, Waddesdon, Bkm
Waddeton Court, Stoke Gabriel, Dev
Waddington Old Hall, Waddington, Yks
Waddow Hall, Waddington, Yks
Wadhurst Hall, Tidebrook, Ssx
Wadley Manor, Wadley, Brk
Wakefield Lodge, Potterspury, Nth
Wakehurst Place, Ardingly, Ssx
Wakes Colne Hall, Wakes Colne, Ess
Walcot Hall, Alkborough, Lin
Walcot Hall, Barnack, Nth
Walcot, Lydbury North, Sal
Waldershare Park, Waldershare, Ken
Walford Hall, Baschurch, Sal
Walford House, West Monkton, Som
Walford Manor, Baschurch, Sal
Walhampton House, Boldre, Ham
Walkern Hall, Walkern, Hrt
Wall Hall, Aldenham, Hrt
Walland Cary, Bucks Mills, Dev
Wallhurst Manor, Cowfold, Ssx
Wallingford Castle, Wallingford, Brk
Wallington Hall, Wallington, Nfk
Wallington, Morpeth, Nbl
Wallingtons, Kintbury, Brk
Walliscote, Whitchurch, Oxf
Wallop Hall, Westbury, Sal
Walls (The), Muncaster, Cul
Wallsworth Hall, Sandhurst, Gls
Walmsgate Hall, Walmsgate, Lin

Walreddon, Whitchurch, Dev
Walshaw Hall, Tottington, Lan
Walsingham Abbey, Little Walsingham, Nfk
Walton Elm, Marnhull, Dor
Walton Hall, Eccleshall, Sts
Walton Hall, Walton, Bkm
Walton Hall, Walton, Chs
Walton Hall, Walton le Dale, Lan
Walton Hall, Walton on Trent, Dby
Walton Hall, Walton, War
Walton Hall, Warrington, Lan
Walton House, Ashchurch, Gls
Walton Lodge, Walton, Dby
Walton Manor, Walton on the Hill, Sry
Waltons, Ashdon, Ess
Walworth Castle, Heighington, Dur
Wanlip Hall, Wanlip, Lei
Wansfell, Ambleside, Wes
Waplington Manor, Allerthorpe, Yks
Wappenbury Hall, Wappenbury, War
Warborne, Boldre, Ham
Warborough House, Stiffkey, Nfk
Warcop Hall, Warcop, Wes
Wardour Castle, Tisbury, Wil
Ware Park, Ware, Hrt
Waren House, Bamburgh, Nbl
Warennes Wood, Stratfield Mortimer, Brk
Waresley Hall, Waresley, Hun
Waresley House, Hartlebury, Wor
Waresley Park, Waresley, Hun
Warfield Hall, Warfield, Brk
Warfield House, Warfield, Brk
Warfield Park, Warfield, Brk
Wargrave Court, Wargrave, Brk
Wargrave Manor, Wargrave, Brk
Warleigh Manor, Bathford, Som
Warleigh, Tamerton Foliot, Dev
Warmwell House, Warmwell, Dor
Warnborough Manor House, South Warnborough, Ham
Warneford Place, Sevenhampton, Wil
Warnford Park, Warnford, Ham
Warnham Court, Warnham, Ssx
Warnham Lodge, Warnham, Ssx
Warren (The), Lower Beeding, Ssx
Warrens, Bramshaw, Ham
Warslow Hall, Warslow, Sts
Warter Priory, Warter, Yks
Wartnaby Hall, Wartnaby, Lei
Warwick Castle, Warwick, War
Warwick Hall, Warwick, Cul
Wasdale Hall, Nether Wasdale, Cul
Washingley Hall, Washingley, Hun
Wasing Place, Wasing, Brk
Wassand Hall, Sigglesthorne, Yks
Wast Hills, Alvechurch, Wor
Watergate House, Upmarden, Ssx
Watermouth Castle, Berrynarbor, Dev
Waterperry House, Waterperry, Oxf
Waterston Manor, Puddletown, Dor
Waterton House, Harnhill, Gls

Watford Court, Watford, Nth
Watlington Hall, Watlington, Nfk
Watlington Park, Watlington, Oxf
Watnall Hall, Watnall, Ntt
Wattlefield Hall, Wattlefield, Nfk
Watts House, Bishops Lydeard, Som
Wavendon House, Wavendon, Bkm
Wavendon Tower, Wavendon, Bkm
Waverley Abbey, Waverley, Sry
Wayton, Landulph, Con
Weald Hall, South Weald, Ess
Weardale Manor, Brasted, Ken
Weare Hall, Weare Gifford, Dev
Weasenham, Weasenham All Saints, Nfk
Weatheroak Hall, Wythall, Wor
Weeting Hall, Weeting, Nfk
Welbeck Abbey, Welbeck, Ntt
Welburn Hall, Kirkdale, Yks
Welford Park, Welford, Brk
Welham Hall, Norton, Yks
Well Close, Brockworth, Gls
Well Hall, Eltham, Ken
Well Vale, Well, Lin
Wellbrook Manor, Peterchurch, Hef
Wellingore Hall, Wellingore, Lin
Wells Palace, Wells, Som
Wellwood, Bardsea, Lan
Welton Manor, Welton le Wold, Lin
Welton Manor, Welton, Nth
Welton Place, Welton, Nth
Wembury House, Wembury, Dev
Wennington Hall, Wennington, Lan
Wensley Hall, Wensley, Yks
Wentworth Castle, Stainborough, Yks
Wentworth Woodhouse, Wentworth, Yks
Wergs Hall, Tettenhall, Sts
Werrington Park, Werrington, Dev
Wessington Court, Woolhope, Hef
West Acre High House, West Acre, Nfk
West Ashby Grove, West Ashby, Lin
West Ashby House, West Ashby, Lin
West Ashby Manor House, West Ashby, Lin
West Bilney Hall, West Bilney, Nfk
West Broyle, Lavant, Ssx
West Cliff Hall, Dibden, Ham
West Coker House, West Coker, Som
West Coker Manor House, West Coker, Som
West Dean Park, West Dean, Ssx
West Farleigh Hall, West Farleigh, Ken
West Felton Grange, West Felton, Sal
West Grinstead Park, West Grinstead, Ssx
West Haddon Hall, West Haddon, Nth
West Hall, High Legh, Chs
West Harling Hall, West Harling, Nfk
West Heslerton Hall, Heslerton, Yks
West Horsley Place, West Horsley, Sry
West Leake Manor, West Leake, Ntt
West Leigh, Havant, Ham
West Lodge, Bradfield St George, Sfk
West Monkton House, West Monkton, Som

West Park, Rockbourne, Ham
West Stoke House, West Stoke, Ssx
West Stowell House, Alton Priors, Wil
West Tisted Manor House, West Tisted, Ham
West Woodhay House, West Woodhay, Brk
West Wratting Hall, West Wratting, Cam
West Wycombe Park, West Wycombe, Bkm
Westbrook Hay, Bovingdon, Hrt
Westbrook, Warnham, Ssx
Westergate Wood, Aldingbourne, Ssx
Westfield Place, Westfield, Ssx
Westholme, Sleaford, Lin
Westhorpe Hall, Southwell, Ntt
Weston Birt House, Weston Birt, Gls
Weston Coyney Hall, Caverswall, Sts
Weston Hall, Bulkington, War
Weston Hall, Weston, Nth
Weston House, Long Compton, War
Weston House, Weston Longville, Nfk
Weston Manor, Totland, Ham
Weston on the Green Manor House, Weston
    on the Green, Oxf
Weston Park, Weston under Lizard, Sts
Weston Turville Manor House, Weston Turville, Bkm
Westoning Manor, Westoning, Bdf
Westwick House, Westwick, Nfk
Westwood Manor, Wetley Rocks, Sts
Westwood Park, Great Horkesley, Ess
Westwood Park, Westwood Park, Wor
Wetherby Grange, Wetherby, Yks
Wetheringsett Manor, Wetheringsett, Sfk
Wethersfield Manor House, Wethersfield, Ess
Wethersfield Place, Wethersfield, Ess
Wetley Abbey, Wetley Rocks, Sts
Wexham Park, Wexham, Bkm
Whaddon Hall, Whaddon, Bkm
Whaddon Manor, Whaddon, Gls
Whatcombe House, Winterbourne Whitechurch, Dor
Whatley House, Whatley, Som
Whatton House, Whatton, Lei
Wheaton Aston Hall, Lapley, Sts
Wheler Lodge, Husbands Bosworth, Lei
Whelprigg, Barbon, Wes
Wherstead Park, Wherstead, Sfk
Wherwell Priory, Wherwell, Ham
Whiddon Park, Chagford, Dev
Whiligh, Ticehurst, Ssx
Whilton Lodge, Whilton, Nth
Whitacre House, Over Whitacre, War
Whitbourne Court, Whitbourne, Hef
Whitbourne Hall, Whitbourne, Hef
Whitburn Hall, Whitburn, Dur
Whitby Hall, Whitby, Chs
White Court, Black Notley, Ess
White Hall (The), Hardingham, Nfk
White Holme, Slaidburn, Yks
White House, Greenwich, Ken
White House (The), Deddington, Oxf
White Lodge, Richmond, Sry
White Waltham Place, White Waltham, Brk

Whitechapel Manor, Bishops Nympton, Dev
Whitefield, Ireby, Cul
Whitehall, Allhallows, Cul
Whitehayes, Burton, Ham
Whitehill, Newton Abbot, Dev
Whitemead Park, Parkend, Gls
Whitestaunton Manor, Whitestaunton, Som
Whiteway, Chudleigh, Dev
Whitfield Hall, Whitfield, Nbl
Whitfield House, Whitfield, Dby
Whitfield, Treville, Hef
Whitgift Hall, Reedness, Yks
Whitley Abbey, Coventry, War
Whitminster House, Whitminster, Gls
Whitmore Hall, Whitmore, Sts
Whitney Court, Whitney, Hef
Whittingham House, Whittingham, Lan
Whittington Court, Whittington, Gls
Whittington Hall, Whittington, Lan
Whittington Old Hall, Whittington, Sts
Whittlebury Lodge, Whittlebury, Nth
Whitton Court, Burford, Sal
Whitton Hall, Westbury, Sal
Whitwell Hall, Whitwell on the Hill, Yks
Whitworth Park, Whitworth, Dur
Whooff House, Aglionby, Cul
Whyly, East Hoathly, Ssx
Wick Court, Wick, Gls
Wick Hall, Radley, Brk
Wick House, Wick, Wor
Wicken Park, Wicken, Nth
Wickham Lodge, Wickham, Ham
Widdicombe, Stokenham, Dev
Widey Court, Egg Buckland, Dev
Widmerpool Hall, Widmerpool, Ntt
Widworthy Court, Widworthy, Dev
Wierton Place, Boughton Monchelsea, Ken
Wiganthorpe, Terrington, Yks
Wigginton Lodge, Tamworth, Sts
Wighill Park, Wighill, Yks
Wigmore, Capel, Sry
Wigmore Hall, Wigmore, Hef
Wigwell Grange, Wirksworth, Dby
Wilbraham-Temple, Great Wilbraham, Cam
Wilburton Manor House, Wilburton, Cam
Wilbury House, Newton Tony, Wil
Wilcote House, North Leigh, Oxf
Wilcote Manor House, Wilcote, Oxf
Wilcroft, Lugwardine, Hef
Wilderness (The), Earley, Brk
Willaston Hall, Willaston, Chs
Willesleigh House, Landkey, Dev
Willesley House, Sherston, Wil
Willestrew House, Lamerton, Dev
Willett House, Elworthy, Som
Willey Hall, Willey, Sal
Williamscote House, Wardington, Oxf
Williamstrip Park, Coln St Aldwyns, Gls
Willingham House, North Willingham, Lin
Willinghurst, Wonersh, Sry

INDEX OF ENGLISH COUNTRY HOUSES

Willington Hall, Willington, Chs
Wilsford Manor, Wilsford, Wil
Wilsic Hall, Stainton, Yks
Wilton House, Wilton, Wil
Wilton Park, Beaconsfield, Bkm
Wilton Place, Dymock, Gls
Wilverley Park, Lyndhurst, Ham
Wimbish Manor House, Shepreth, Cam
Wimblehurst, Horsham, Ssx
Wimbolds Trafford Hall, Wimbolds Trafford, Chs
Wimpole Hall, Wimpole, Cam
Winchester House, Putney, Sry
Winchfield House, Winchfield, Ham
Winchfield Lodge, Winchfield, Ham
Wincombe Park, Donhead St Mary, Wil
Windebrow, Underskiddaw, Cul
Winderwath, Cliburn, Wes
Windlesham Court, Windlesham, Sry
Windmill Hill House, Hampstead, Mdx
Windmill Hill Place, Wartling, Ssx
Winford Manor, Winford, Som
Wing Grange, Wing, Rut
Wingfield House, Wingfield, Wil
Wingfield Park, South Wingfield, Dby
Wingrave Old Manor House, Wingrave, Bkm
Winkburn Hall, Winkburn, Ntt
Winkleigh Court, Winkleigh, Dev
Winmarleigh Hall, Winmarleigh, Lan
Winslade, Clyst St Mary, Dev
Winsley Hall, Westbury, Sal
Winsley Hurst, Hartwith, Yks
Winslow Hall, Winslow, Bkm
Winstanley Hall, Billinge Chapel End, Lan
Winterdyne, Bewdley, Wor
Winterfold, Chaddesley Corbett, Wor
Wintershill Hall, Upham, Ham
Winthorpe Hall, Winthorpe, Ntt
Winwick Manor, Winwick, Nth
Wirswall Hall, Wirswall, Chs
Wiscombe Park, Southleigh, Dev
Wiseton Hall, Wiseton, Ntt
Wistaston Hall, Wistaston, Chs
Wiston Park, Wiston, Ssx
Wistow Hall, Wistow, Lei
Witchingham Hall, Great Witchingham, Nfk
Witcombe Park, Witcombe, Gls
Witham Hall, Witham on the Hill, Lin
Witham Lodge, Witham, Ess
Withcote Hall, Withcote, Lei
Witherdon, Broadwood Widger, Dev
Withersdane Hall, Wye, Ken
Witherslack Hall, Witherslack, Wes
Withington Hall, Old Withington, Chs
Withnell Fold, Withnell, Lan
Witley Court, Great Witley, Wor
Witley Park, Witley, Sry
Wittington, Medmenham, Bkm
Witton Castle, Witton le Wear, Dur
Witton Park, Blackburn, Lan
Wivenhoe Park, Wivenhoe, Ess

Wiverton Hall, Tithby, Ntt
Wiveton Hall, Wiveton, Nfk
Woburn Abbey, Woburn, Bdf
Wodehouse (The), Wombourn, Sts
Wold Newton Hall, Wold Newton, Yks
Wold Newton Manor, Wold Newton, Lin
Woldhurstlea, Ifield, Ssx
Woldringfold, Cowfold, Ssx
Wolford Lodge, Dunkeswell, Dev
Wolhayes, Highcliff, Ham
Wolsdon, Antony, Con
Wolseley Hall, Colwich, Sts
Wolston Grange, Wolston, War
Wolterton Park, Wolterton, Nfk
Wolverley Court, Wolverley, Wor
Wolverley House, Wolverley, Wor
Wolverton Park, Wolverton, Ham
Wolvey Hall, Wolvey, War
Wolviston Hall, Wolviston, Dur
Womersley Park, Womersley, Yks
Wonastow Court, Wonastow, Mon
Wonham, Bampton, Dev
Wooburn House, Wooburn, Bkm
Wood Broughton, Field Broughton, Lan
Wood Eaton Manor, Wood Eaton, Oxf
Wood Hall, Arkesden, Ess
Wood Hall, Bridekirk, Cul
Wood Hall, Hilgay, Nfk
Wood Hall, Kirkby Overblow, Yks
Wood Hall, Norton by Kempsey, Wor
Wood Hall, Sutton, Sfk
Wood Hill, Gressenhall, Nfk
Wood Hill, Trefonen, Sal
Wood Rising Hall, Woodrising, Nfk
Wood, South Tawton, Dev
Woodbastwick Hall, Woodbastwick, Nfk
Woodborough Green, Camerton, Som
Woodborough Hall, Woodborough, Ntt
Woodbridge Abbey, Woodbridge, Sfk
Woodbury Hall, Gamlingay, Cam
Woodcote Grove, Epsom, Sry
Woodcote Hall, Woodcote, Sal
Woodcote House, Epsom, Sry
Woodcote, Leek Wootton, War
Woodcote Manor, Bramdean, Ham
Woodcroft Castle, Etton, Nth
Woodend, Thornthwaite, Cul
Woodfold Park, Mellor, Lan
Woodford House, Woodford near Thrapston, Nth
Woodhill, Sandon, Ess
Woodhouse, Olveston, Gls
Woodhouse, Uplyme, Dev
Woodhouse, West Felton, Sal
Woodlands, Aislaby, Yks
Woodlands, Chelsfield, Ken
Woodlands Hall, Glazeley, Sal
Woodlands House, Netley Marsh, Ham
Woodlands, Kenn, Dev
Woodlands (The), Greenwich, Ken
Woodlands Vale, Ryde, Ham

INDEX OF ENGLISH COUNTRY HOUSES

Woodleys, Wootton, Oxf
Woodmancote Place, Woodmancote, Ssx
Woodmanton Manor, Clifton on Teme, Wor
Woodperry, Stanton St John, Oxf
Woodredon, Waltham Abbey, Ess
Woodrow High House, Amersham, Bkm
Woodseat, Rocester, Sts
Woodside House, Chenies, Bkm
Woodspring Priory, Kewstoke, Som
Woodstock, Tunstall, Ken
Woodthorpe Hall, Woodthorpe Strubby, Lin
Woolas Hall, Eckington, Wor
Woolbeding House, Woolbeding, Ssx
Woolhampton Park, Woolhampton, Brk
Woolland House, Woolland, Dor
Woolley Park, Chaddleworth, Brk
Woolley Park, Woolley, Yks
Woolmer Lodge, Bramshott, Ham
Woolmers, Hertingfordbury, Hrt
Woolston, Loddiswell, Dev
Woolverstone Park, Woolverstone, Sfk
Wootton Court, Leek Wootton, War
Wootton Fitzpaine Manor House, Wootton Fitzpaine,
    Dor
Wootton Hall, Wootton, Lin
Wootton Hall, Wootton Wawen, War
Wootton House, Wootton, Bdf
Wootton Lodge, Ellastone, Sts
Wootton Manor, Folkington, Ssx
Worden, Leyland, Lan
Workington Hall, Workington, Cul
Worksop Manor House, Worksop, Ntt
Wormhill Hall, Wormhill, Dby
Wormington Grange, Stanton, Gls
Wormley Bury, Wormley, Hrt
Wormsley, Stokenchurch, Bkm
Wormstall, Kintbury, Brk
Worstead House, Worstead, Nfk
Worth House, Washfield, Dev
Wortham Manor, Wortham, Sfk
Worthy Park, Martyr Worthy, Ham
Worting House, Worting, Ham
Wortley Hall, Wortley, Yks
Wotton House, Wotton, Sry
Wotton House, Wotton Underwood, Bkm
Woughton House, Woughton on the Green, Bkm
Wraxall Court, Wraxall, Som
Wray Castle, Wray, Lan
Wrea Head, Scalby, Yks
Wreay Hall, Wreay, Cul
Wrelton Hall, Middleton, Yks
Wrentnall House, Church Pulverbatch, Sal
Wretham Hall, West Wretham, Nfk
Wrightington Hall, Wrightington, Lan

Wrotham Hill Park, Wrotham, Ken
Wrotham Park, Potters Bar, Mdx
Wrottesley Hall, Tettenhall, Sts
Wroxall Abbey, Wroxall, War
Wroxham Hall, Wroxham, Nfk
Wroxham House, Wroxham, Nfk
Wroxton Abbey, Wroxton, Oxf
Wyastone Leys, Dixton, Mon
Wyastone Leys, Ganarew, Hef
Wychbold Hall, Wychbold, Wor
Wychnor Park, Wichnor, Sts
Wycliffe Hall, Wycliffe, Yks
Wydale, Brompton, Yks
Wyddial Hall, Wyddial, Hrt
Wyelands, Mathern, Mon
Wyfold Court, Checkendon, Oxf
Wyke Hall, Gillingham, Dor
Wykeham Abbey, Wykeham with Ruston, Yks
Wyken Hall, Bardwell, Sfk
Wykham Park, Banbury, Oxf
Wyld Court, Hawkchurch, Dev
Wyldes, Hampstead, Mdx
Wyllyotts Manor, Potters Bar, Mdx
Wymondley House, Little Wymondley, Hrt
Wyndthorpe, Hatfield, Yks
Wynyard Park, Grindon, Dur
Wyphurst, Cranleigh, Sry
Wyresdale Park, Scorton, Lan
Wythall, Walford, Hef
Wytham Abbey, Wytham, Brk

Yaldham Manor, Wrotham, Ken
Yarlington House, Yarlington, Som
Yarner, Bovey Tracey, Dev
Yarrow Hall, Bintree, Nfk
Yate House, Yate, Gls
Yate Lawn, Yate, Gls
Yattendon Court, Yattendon, Brk
Yattendon House, Frilsham, Brk
Yatton Court, Aymestrey, Hef
Yaverland Manor House, Yaverland, Ham
Yaxley Hall, Yaxley, Sfk
Yeaton-Peverey, Baschurch, Sal
Yeldersley Hall, Yeldersley, Dby
Yewden Manor, Hambleden, Bkm
Yokefleet Hall, Laxton, Yks
Yokes Court, Frinsted, Ken
York Cottage, Sandringham, Nfk
Yotes Court, Mereworth, Ken
Youlbury, Boar's Hill, Brk
Youlston Park, Shirwell, Dev
Youngsbury, High Cross, Hrt

Zeals House, Zeals, Wil